Empower Children Through Play Therapy!

Practical Guide, Fun Strategies to Engage Your Child, Boost Confidence, Promote Positive Behaviors, and Enhance Resilience with Culturally Diverse Activities for Well-Being.

This book is fondly dedicated to my loving husband for your unwavering support and to LC. This work is in support of dedicated therapists such as yourself. Love always,

~ Deana.

Table of Contents

Introduction

As you open this book, you're not just beginning to read another text about therapy; you're stepping onto a path that leads toward transformative healing and empowerment for children. Play therapy is more than a set of techniques—it's a journey of discovery, connection, and growth that holds the potential to reshape young lives profoundly.

My journey into the heart of play therapy began through a blend of professional curiosity and personal necessity. Witnessing adults' struggles in guiding children through emotional and behavioral challenges, I was drawn to the power of play as a therapeutic tool. This book springs from a deep commitment to providing you—parents, caregivers, and therapists—with practical, accessible strategies that can truly make a difference.

"Empower Children Through Play Therapy" is crafted to distill the complexities of therapeutic play into practical, enjoyable activities that address and celebrate cultural diversity. These strategies are designed to foster positive behavior, boost resilience, and enhance the overall well-being of children.

You, the reader, are likely a part of a dynamic group of adults aged 25-45. Whether you're a seasoned therapist, a new parent, or a caregiver, this guide is tailored to meet your needs with innovative, evidence-based solutions. It's constructed to resonate with those who seek to apply therapeutic techniques and weave them seamlessly into everyday interactions with children.

This book directly addresses the most common concerns identified in extensive customer research. It focuses on inclusivity, practical relevance, and the unique challenges you face in nurturing children in today's world. Each chapter builds incrementally on the last, equipping you with a comprehensive toolkit that evolves from basic principles to advanced applications of play therapy.

Grounded in robust research and current best practices, the strategies you will learn are scientifically supported and honed by real-world applications. You prepare to understand and effectively implement strategies to transform lives as you turn each page.

Please engage with this material as a reader and actively participate in a transformative process. This journey will enhance your skills and strategies as a caregiver or therapist and deepen your connections with the children in your care, enriching your relationships and offering new insights into the therapeutic power of play.

As we embark on this journey together, remember that the ultimate goal of this book is to empower you to bring healing, joy, and resilience into the lives of children. Let's begin this hopeful, empowering journey together, with every page you turn and every strategy you apply, bringing you closer to understanding the full potential of play therapy in changing young lives for the better.

Chapter 1

Foundations of Play Therapy

Have you ever observed children lost in the throes of imaginative play, perhaps constructing elaborate fantasy worlds, dialoguing with invisible friends, or molding shapes from the sand? There's a raw, transformative power in these moments of play - a power that goes beyond mere amusement. Play isn't just a pastime for children experiencing emotional or behavioral challenges; it's a vital pathway to healing and growth. This is the heartland of play therapy, where structured play becomes a dynamic force, facilitating communication, expression, and healing in ways words cannot consistently achieve.

Here, we explore the foundational aspects of play therapy, understanding its purpose, significance in development, operational environments, and the core goals that guide its practice.

1.1 What is Play Therapy? Understanding Its Role in Child Development

Play therapy is a distinct psychotherapeutic approach designed for children primarily to explore their lives and express thoughts and emotions that might be repressed or unarticulated in everyday interactions. While play is a natural part of childhood, therapeutic play is carefully guided. It differs from regular play in its intentionality; it is structured and directed by a trained therapist to create a safe, constructive space for expression and learning. Through play therapy, toys become tools and play scenarios transform into insightful narratives that help therapists understand and address a child's inner world.

The developmental significance of play extends across various domains—physical, social, emotional, and cognitive. For instance, when children engage in physical play activities, they are enhancing their motor skills and learning boundaries, the capabilities of their bodies, and the fundamentals of self-care. Socially, play involves interaction rules and turn-taking, foundational elements that foster interpersonal skills and empathy. Emotionally, play allows children to experiment with different outcomes, experiencing both frustration and success, which can lead to enhanced emotional resilience. Cognitively, play supports language development as children negotiate roles, articulate rules, or converse with play partners, enriching their vocabulary and linguistic structures.

The environments in which play therapy occurs are as critical as the activities themselves. Whether in schools, where therapists can observe and interact within the child's social domain, in clinics explicitly designed for therapeutic interventions, or in-home therapy rooms that provide comfort and familiarity, each setting plays a vital role in the effectiveness of the therapy. These controlled environments are meticulously prepared to ensure safety, confidentiality, and the therapeutic alignment of physical space with treatment goals.

The overarching goals of play therapy are tailored to meet each child's developmental needs and personal circumstances. Common objectives include:

- Reducing anxiety, often involves exercises to control external elements within the play.
- Providing emotional support through the security of predictable and empathetic interactions.
- Developing coping mechanisms, where children learn to identify and manage emotions or scenarios that might occur in their everyday lives.

These goals shift depending on the child's age, developmental stage, and specific emotional or behavioral needs, ensuring that the therapy grows with the child.

Interactive Element: Reflective Journal Prompt

Consider the role of play in your childhood. Reflect on a moment where play taught you something significant about yourself or the world. How might these insights help you understand the therapeutic potential of play for children facing emotional or behavioral challenges?

By delving into these foundational elements of play therapy, you gain an awareness of its techniques and settings and a deeper appreciation of how play can be a profound tool for healing and development. As we explore more specific applications and benefits of play therapy in subsequent sections, remember these core principles that support and justify its use in therapeutic settings.

1.2 The Therapeutic Powers of Play: How Play Facilitates Healing and Growth

Play therapy, at its core, is a conduit for expression and healing, addressing emotional and psychological challenges that children may not be able to articulate through conventional communication. The mechanisms of healing within play therapy are deeply rooted in psychological theories that underscore the importance of expression in the developmental process. Projection and internalization are two such mechanisms that frequently come into play. Projection allows children to transfer their feelings or experiences onto objects or characters in their play. For instance, a child might express sadness by having a puppet act out a story of loneliness. This provides a safe psychological distance from their feelings, allowing them to deal with complex emotions in a manageable way. Internalization occurs when children absorb the experiences from play and integrate them into their understanding of the world and themselves, often reshaping previously held negative perceptions or fears.

To illustrate, let's consider several case studies where play therapy has been instrumental in facilitating significant emotional healing and developmental progress. In one documented instance, a child who had experienced severe anxiety following a family tragedy began to reenact the event through play. Over time, guided by a skilled therapist, the child's play evolved from replaying the traumatic event to introducing new outcomes where help arrived, demonstrating a shift from a sense of helplessness to one of hope and resilience. Another case involved a young girl who struggled with attachment issues due to early neglect. Through doll play, she expressed care and attachment, gradually mirroring these behaviors in her interactions with caregivers, thus enhancing her ability to form healthy relationships.

The role of play in brain development is another critical aspect, where neural pathways associated with various cognitive functions such as creativity, problem-solving, and interpersonal skills are significantly stimulated. Children often encounter scenarios that require innovative thinking and problem resolution during play. For example, building a bridge out of blocks that keep collapsing teaches a child about gravity, balance, and spatial relationships, engaging cognitive processes fundamental in STEM (science, technology, engineering, and mathematics) learning. Moreover, play settings that require children to negotiate roles or rules enhance their linguistic abilities and social cognition, preparing them for complex interpersonal interactions and collaborations.

Empirical support for the therapeutic benefits of play is robust and sourced from many studies and clinical observations. Research consistently shows that play therapy can improve children's emotional well-being, social behaviors, and cognitive abilities. For instance, a meta-analysis of play therapy outcomes indicated significant positive effects across various therapeutic settings, irrespective of the child's gender, age, or the specific nature of their emotional or psychological challenges. These studies underscore play therapy's effectiveness as a supportive therapeutic approach and a critical, evidence-based practice integral to child psychology.

Understanding these foundational aspects of how play therapy facilitates healing and growth allows us to appreciate its potential in rectifying developmental challenges and promoting a holistic developmental trajectory for children facing various psychological hurdles. As we continue to explore and implement play therapy, these insights guide our practices, ensuring that each child's unique needs and potentials are addressed with scientifically-backed strategies and a heart geared towards nurturing and understanding.

1.3 Key Principles of Play Therapy: A Guide to Techniques and Applications

At the heart of effective play therapy lies core principles that guide the therapeutic process, ensuring it is respectful, targeted, and conducive to the child's development. These foundational principles include child-centered therapy, the therapist's role as a facilitator, and creating a safe and confidential environment. Each of these principles plays a pivotal role in the success of the therapy, crafting a space where children can freely express themselves and explore their emotions without fear of judgment or repercussion.

Child-centered therapy is the cornerstone of play therapy, emphasizing the importance of viewing the therapeutic process through the child's eyes and experiences. This approach allows the therapy to be guided by the child's needs, interests, and developmental stage rather than strictly directed by the therapist. This principle respects the child's pace and natural inclinations, which can lead to more genuine and spontaneous expressions during play. It facilitates a more profound understanding by the therapist of the child's worldview, enhancing the ability to tailor meaningful and effective interventions.

The therapist's role as a facilitator is crucial. Unlike traditional therapy models where the therapist may lead the session, in play therapy, the therapist often takes a step back, allowing the child to lead the way. This non-directive approach helps to empower the child, giving them control over the play and, by extension, their healing process. The therapist's primary role becomes observation, understanding, and subtle guidance, helping unlock the therapeutic messages hidden within the child's play. The skills required for this role are unique — patience, empathy, and a keen ability to interpret non-verbal cues are essential. These attributes help the therapist to remain attuned to the child's needs and respond in a way that promotes further exploration and development.

The environment in which play therapy takes place also significantly impacts its effectiveness. A safe and confidential setting is imperative. This not only refers to the physical safety of the environment but also to the emotional and psychological safety of the child. Children must feel secure and know that the boundaries of their therapeutic space are respected and maintained. Confidentiality is critical to fostering a trusting relationship between the child and the therapist, encouraging open and honest expression through play.

Diving deeper into the techniques used in play therapy, we find various creative and engaging methods such as sand play, role-play, and storytelling. Each technique has its unique function and is chosen based on its suitability to the child's specific issues and therapeutic goals.

Sand play, for instance, allows children to create and manipulate a miniature world using various figures and elements in a sandbox. This can be particularly therapeutic for children who may feel overwhelmed by real-world situations, as it gives them a sense of control and the ability to externalize complex feelings in a manageable, contained space.

Role-play is another powerful technique, allowing children to experiment with different roles and outcomes in a safe setting. This can be particularly effective in helping children develop problem-solving skills, understand social norms, and work through interpersonal conflicts. It provides a stage for children to express feelings, adopt different perspectives, and experiment with various responses to see their consequences.

Whether led by the child or the therapist, storytelling is a profoundly symbolic medium that can help children articulate experiences and emotions they might not otherwise express. Through stories, children can distance themselves from painful experiences, which can be particularly useful in cases of trauma. The narrative form helps them reframe their experiences and often leads to a greater sense of resolution and understanding.

In application, these techniques are adapted to fit various therapeutic scenarios. For instance, in dealing with trauma, storytelling, and sand play can help children process and narrate their experiences in a symbolic form, making the trauma more manageable. Role-play can effectively teach social skills and better ways to express emotions in behavioral issues. Family dysfunction might be approached through group play therapy sessions, where family members engage in "play" to improve communication, understanding, and emotional bonds within the family unit.

Each of these principles, techniques, and applications is interwoven to form a comprehensive approach to play therapy, one that respects and responds to each child's individual needs. As we continue to explore and apply these foundational elements, we enhance our ability to provide a therapeutic experience that is effective and transformative, allowing children to navigate their developmental paths with resilience and emotional intelligence.

1.4 Setting Up for Success: Creating an Effective Play Therapy Environment

Creating an environment conducive to effective play therapy is akin to setting the stage for a transformative play production, where every element—be it the props (toys and materials) or the script (therapeutic techniques)—plays a pivotal role in facilitating the child's journey towards emotional and psychological healing. The design of a play therapy room should be intentional, promoting a sense of safety and creativity while being adaptive to meet the diverse needs of each child. In this regard, thoughtful consideration of the types of toys and materials included and the overall layout can significantly influence the therapeutic process.

When considering room design, selecting versatile and open-ended toys to encourage a broad spectrum of emotional expression and cognitive exploration is essential. Items such as dolls, building blocks, art supplies, and dress-up costumes allow children to create and manipulate their environments symbolically, which can be crucial for expressing complex emotions and scenarios. The room layout should provide clear, open spaces for active play and quieter corners for reflective activities. This spatial arrangement helps manage the flow of the session and mirrors the dynamic range of emotional and cognitive experiences that play therapy seeks to encompass. Additionally, ensuring that the room is free from clutter and organized so that children can choose and return items independently fosters a sense of autonomy and responsibility, enhancing their engagement and the therapeutic alliance.

Safety within the play therapy environment extends beyond physical safety to emotional and psychological security. This dual focus on safety is critical because the effectiveness of play therapy hinges on the child's sense of security and trust in the therapeutic environment. Physically, the room should be equipped with safe, non-toxic materials and furniture with rounded edges to prevent accidents. Emotionally and psychologically, the space must be arranged to feel private and contained, where children understand that their communications are confidential and that the space is a sanctuary from outside judgments or expectations. This sense of bounded safety can be reinforced by soundproofing the room where possible and discussing with children the people who might have access to the information shared during therapy, such as caregivers or medical professionals, under specific, explained circumstances.

Creating an inclusive environment that acknowledges and respects cultural, social, and personal backgrounds is crucial in making play therapy effective for all children. This involves more than just having a diverse array of dolls or books; it means creating a space that feels welcoming and affirming of different identities. For instance, including materials that reflect various cultural backgrounds, languages, and family structures helps in fostering an environment where all children feel seen and understood. Moreover, therapists should be mindful of using décor and play materials that are not only culturally inclusive but also sensitive to children from different religious or spiritual backgrounds, ensuring that these elements are used in ways that respect their intrinsic values and meanings.

Adapting the play therapy environment to accommodate children with special needs, such as sensory integration issues or physical disabilities, is also fundamental. This might involve incorporating sensory-friendly materials, such as noise-canceling headphones for children with auditory sensitivities, or ensuring the space is accessible for children with mobility aids. For children who are easily overwhelmed by sensory input, creating a corner of the room with dimmed lighting and calming sensory objects like soft rugs, cushions, or a tent can provide a necessary retreat. For those requiring physical accommodations, the layout should allow for unobstructed movement, and furniture should be adaptable to meet different bodily needs. By anticipating and planning for these needs, the therapy environment becomes a place where all children can engage meaningfully, regardless of their physical or sensory capabilities.

The overarching goal of setting up a play therapy room is to create a space that champions the child's needs and promotes therapeutic goals through thoughtful, inclusive design and safety-oriented practices. Such environments support the specific play therapy modalities and contribute to a broader sense of acceptance and understanding, foundational to practical therapy sessions. By meticulously designing this space, therapists can significantly enhance the therapeutic journey, making each session an opportunity for profound emotional and developmental growth.

1.5 Play Therapy Across Cultures: Ensuring Sensitivity and Inclusivity

In play therapy, cultural competence is essential, reflecting a therapist's ability to understand, appreciate, and integrate a child's cultural background into their therapeutic practices. Cultural competence in play therapy involves more than just an awareness of diverse cultural expressions; it requires an active engagement and sensitivity to the cultural values, beliefs, and practices that shape children's experiences and identities. This understanding is crucial because each child's cultural background significantly influences how they perceive the world, respond to challenges, and communicate their thoughts and feelings. By integrating these cultural nuances into play therapy, therapists can create a more inclusive and effective therapeutic environment that resonates deeply with the child's lived experiences, enhancing the therapeutic alliance and outcomes.

One of the most potent aspects of culturally competent play therapy is its capacity to adapt techniques to honor and reflect the diverse needs of children from various backgrounds. For instance, consider the use of storytelling in play therapy. A therapist working with a child from a Native American background might incorporate traditional tribal stories that carry essential cultural teachings and values. This validates the child's cultural heritage and uses familiar narratives that the child can relate to deeply, making the therapeutic messages more impactful. Similarly, dolls and figurines that reflect the child's racial and ethnic identity can help in role-playing scenarios, making the play more relatable and affirming the child's sense of self and community.

The adaptation of play therapy to meet diverse cultural needs can be seen in various case examples where culturally sensitive interventions have led to significant breakthroughs in therapy sessions. For example, a therapist working with a young refugee from Syria used a sand tray therapy setup to recreate scenes from the child's journey and life before the war. This approach allowed the child to process the trauma and loss experienced during the conflict and displacement in a non-threatening, controlled environment. The therapist carefully introduced elements that symbolized hope and safety, such as figures representing helpers (like doctors and teachers), which the child could place in the scene as desired, gradually introducing a sense of control and resilience into the child's narrative.

For therapists aiming to deepen their cultural competence, a wealth of resources is available that can enhance understanding and skills;

Seminars and workshops designed explicitly around cultural sensitivity in therapeutic practices can provide valuable insights and strategies for integrating cultural awareness into everyday therapy sessions. Books such as "Culturally Alert Counseling: A Comprehensive Introduction" by Garrett McAuliffe and "Developing Multicultural Counseling Competence: A Systems Approach" by Danica G. Hays and Bradley T. Erford offer therapists extensive frameworks and practical advice. Additionally, engaging in peer consultation groups focusing on cultural competence can provide ongoing support and learning, allowing therapists to share experiences, challenges, and successes in implementing culturally sensitive practices.

The journey toward cultural competence is ongoing and evolves with each therapeutic interaction. It requires therapists to be continually reflective, open to learning, and proactive in seeking an understanding of the cultural dynamics that influence their clients' lives. By committing to this level of sensitivity and inclusivity, play therapists enhance their therapeutic effectiveness and contribute to a broader culture of respect, acceptance, and empathy within the therapeutic community and beyond. This commitment ensures that all children feel seen, heard, and valued within their therapeutic journeys, regardless of their cultural, ethnic, or social backgrounds.

1.6 Overcoming Common Misconceptions About Play Therapy

In therapeutic practices, play therapy often encounters misconceptions that can undermine its perceived value and efficacy. A common misapprehension is that play therapy is merely play, lacking the seriousness and impact of more 'traditional' therapeutic approaches. In reality, play therapy is a deeply structured and theoretically grounded approach specifically tailored to help children express and process emotions and experiences that might be inaccessible through traditional verbal therapy methods. Play is the medium through which children can safely explore and express their inner worlds; it is not simply recreational but a vital part of their cognitive and emotional processing.

Another prevalent misconception is that play therapy is exclusively beneficial for very young children. This notion needs to recognize the versatility and adaptability of play therapy, which can be profoundly helpful for various age groups, including adolescents. For younger children, play therapy might involve more literal forms of play, such as using toys or art to express feelings and resolve conflicts. However, play therapy can be adapted with adolescents to include more complex scenarios and role-plays that engage their advanced cognitive and emotional capacities. For example, an adolescent might engage in a role-play that explores future career aspirations or personal relationships, allowing them to address anxieties or expectations pertinent to their developmental stage.

Skepticism often arises about the scope of play therapy's effectiveness, scientific validity, and therapeutic outcomes. It's essential to highlight that the effectiveness of play therapy is well-documented through numerous empirical studies and supported by psychological theories. Longitudinal studies have shown that children who engage in play therapy exhibit long-term improvements in areas such as anxiety reduction, behavior modification, and emotional resilience. The therapeutic success is not anecdotal but is grounded in ongoing, rigorous research that underpins the strategies and techniques used in play therapy settings.

Regarding professional standards, play therapy is a specialized field that requires rigorous training and certification. Play therapists are often licensed mental health professionals who have undergone additional, specific training in play therapy techniques and theories. Various professional bodies, such as the Association for Play Therapy, offer certifications that ensure therapists have met the required educational and clinical experience standards. These certifications are not merely formalities but assurances of the therapist's ability to provide safe, effective, and ethical treatment. Ensuring therapists meet these standards protects the integrity of the therapeutic process and ensures that the children who undergo play therapy receive the highest standard of care.

Therefore, play therapy is a robust, versatile, and professionally recognized therapeutic approach. The client's age does not limit its effectiveness, but it is a dynamic and adaptable tool that can meet children's and adolescents' complex emotional and psychological needs. The professional standards governing its practice ensure that it is delivered with the utmost care and expertise, making it a reliable choice for those seeking therapeutic support for the younger population. As we continue to educate and inform about the nuances and benefits of play therapy, we not only dispel these common misconceptions but also open doors for more children and adolescents to benefit from its healing potential.

Chapter 2

Engaging Techniques for Diverse Needs

Imagine stepping into a room where every item and activity is a gateway to better focus, engagement, and joy for a child. This chapter explores specialized techniques in play therapy designed to cater to children with Attention Deficit Hyperactivity Disorder (ADHD). Children with ADHD often face unique challenges that can impact their ability to engage in traditional learning and play environments. They might struggle with maintaining attention, managing impulsivity, or staying still, which can often lead to feelings of frustration and inadequacy. However, through tailored play therapy strategies, you can transform these challenges into opportunities for growth and joy, allowing these children to constructively harness their energy and creativity.

2.1 Play Therapy for Children with ADHD: Strategies for Engagement and Focus

Structured Play Schedules

For children with ADHD, predictability can be a key to successful engagement in therapy. Structured play schedules are vital because they provide a clear framework for children to operate, reducing anxiety and helping them focus better. Imagine a play session that starts with a welcome ritual, transitions into a high-energy physical activity, then a calming sensory activity, and concludes with a reflective closing ritual. This structure not only helps in managing expectations but also in harnessing the child's strengths at different phases of the session. For instance, starting with physical activities can help a child expend excess energy, making them more receptive to engaging in focused, sit-down activities later. Each session can be visualized as a mini-journey, where the child knows the roadmap and what's expected at each stop, providing them with a sense of security and control.

Activity Rotation

Rotating activities within a play therapy session can significantly enhance engagement for children with ADHD. This strategy involves changing activities to align with the child's natural attention span, which can vary widely among children with ADHD. For example, a session might begin with a 10-minute puzzle, followed by 5 minutes drawing, and then 10 minutes role-playing. The key is to observe and identify the optimal time for activity changes, which might be signaled by the child's body language or verbal cues indicating restlessness or disinterest. By keeping the sessions dynamic and fluid, you cater to the child's need for novelty and stimulation, thereby maintaining their interest and participation throughout the therapy process.

Sensory-Motor Activities

Incorporating sensory-motor activities into play therapy can be particularly beneficial for managing impulsivity and hyperactivity, common characteristics of ADHD. Activities like obstacle courses, rhythm games, or simple tasks like bouncing a ball on a rhythm provide structured ways for children to channel their energy productively. These activities engage both the body and the mind, requiring children to focus on coordination and sensory integration, which can improve their ability to control impulses and maintain attention.

Moreover, these activities can be inherently rewarding, providing immediate feedback and satisfaction and reinforcing positive participation and effort.

Rewards and Incentives

Using rewards and incentives can be an effective strategy to encourage sustained effort and attention from children with ADHD. However, the key to success with this strategy lies in its implementation. Rewards should be immediate and linked directly to specific behaviors or achievements within the session. For example, completing a puzzle might earn a sticker, or maintaining focus for a total activity could result in choosing the next game to play. These rewards must be attainable and frequent enough to motivate the child throughout the session. Additionally, involving the child in setting the goals and choosing the rewards can further enhance their engagement and commitment to the therapy process.

Interactive Element: Goal-Setting Exercise

Consider this interactive exercise, in which you can engage with the child in setting specific, achievable goals for each session as a therapist or caregiver. Use a simple chart or visual aid where these goals and corresponding rewards are clearly outlined. This helps keep the child informed and involved and serves as a motivational tool where they can see their progress and look forward to earning their rewards. This exercise underscores the therapy's collaborative nature, empowering the child to take an active role in their therapeutic journey.

As you apply these strategies, it's important to remember that each child with ADHD is unique, and what works for one might not work for another. Observing, adapting, and personalizing these techniques to fit the individual child's needs and responses is crucial. By doing so, you create a therapeutic environment that not only addresses the challenges of ADHD but also celebrates the child's strengths and potential, fostering an atmosphere of growth, focus, and joy.

2.2 Designing Play Therapy for Children with Autism: Communication and Socialization

When addressing the needs of children with autism in play therapy, the focus intensifies on enhancing communication, fostering socialization, and creating a sensory-sensitive environment. These children often experience the world differently, with unique challenges in understanding and engaging in typical social interactions and communication. You can significantly bridge these gaps by integrating thoughtful tools and structured play scenarios, offering them a better platform to express themselves and connect with others.

Using non-verbal communication tools like Picture Exchange Communication Systems (PECS) or sign language can dramatically enhance the therapy experience for children with autism. PECS allows children to communicate through pictures, which can be particularly effective for those who find verbal communication challenging. This system involves an exchange of pictures to communicate desires, observations, and feelings. For instance, a child could hand a therapist a picture of a swing to indicate a willingness to engage in that activity, thereby bypassing the need for verbal requests, which might be difficult for them. Incorporating sign language as part of play therapy can also be beneficial, especially for children who have better motor than vocal skills. Using simple signs during play activities, like 'more,' 'done,' or 'wait,' can empower the child to communicate effectively and reduce frustrations caused by communication barriers.

Role-playing scenarios are another cornerstone in enhancing communication and social skills. These scenarios can be tailored to real-life situations that a child might find challenging, like a birthday party or a classroom setting. The child can practice and learn social cues and appropriate responses by simulating these environments in a controlled play setting. For example, setting up a birthday party scenario where the child needs to greet guests, thank them for gifts, or take turns in games can provide a rehearsal space for social interactions. The therapist can guide the role-play, prompting the child with cues if necessary, and gradually reduce these prompts as the child becomes more comfortable and adept in these interactions.

Visual supports such as schedules, storyboards, and visual cues also play a critical role in structuring play sessions for children with autism. These tools help lay out the sequence of activities clearly, which helps reduce anxiety about unpredictability—one of the common challenges faced by these children. A visual schedule might outline the order of play activities, with pictures representing each task, such as a picture of a paintbrush followed by a picture of a toy car and then a book. This prepares the child for what's next and helps them transition more easily from one activity to another. Storyboards can narrate a sequence of events or explain the rules of a game, providing a visual script that children can follow.

Sensory sensitivities are a significant consideration when selecting play materials for autistic children. Many children on the autism spectrum may have heightened or reduced responses to sensory stimuli. Therefore, choosing materials that cater to their sensory needs can substantially affect their comfort and engagement levels. For example, using soft textures in costumes or play mats can be soothing for a child who might find hard surfaces uncomfortable.

Similarly, opting for non-fluorescent, natural lighting can help avoid discomfort caused by harsh lighting. The play environment should be audited for potential sensory triggers and adjusted to ensure a welcoming and comfortable space for the child to engage and learn effectively.

By carefully considering and integrating these strategies into play therapy sessions, you create a supportive, engaging, and effective therapeutic environment for children with autism. This not only aids in their communication and social skills development but also respects and accommodates their sensory preferences, overall enhancing their ability to navigate and enjoy their world more fully.

2.3 Trauma-Informed Play Therapy: Techniques for Sensitive Practice

Trauma-informed play therapy is a specialized approach that recognizes and addresses the unique needs of children who have experienced traumatic events. This form of therapy is grounded in the understanding that trauma can profoundly affect a child's emotional, psychological, and physical well-being. Therefore, creating a safe play environment where trust is paramount becomes the cornerstone of therapeutic interaction. Trust in this context is about believing what the child says and building a secure space where they feel valued, understood, and safe to express themselves without fear of judgment or retribution. Methods to establish and maintain this sense of safety include consistent routines within therapy sessions, clear boundaries that are respectfully maintained, and the predictable presence of the therapist as a secure base from which the child can explore and express their feelings.

The significance of allowing children to make choices during play cannot be overstressed, especially for those recovering from trauma. Traumatic experiences often involve situations where the child feels powerless or has no control over what is happening to them. By integrating choice and control into play therapy, you empower the child. Simple decisions like picking which game to play, selecting toys, or choosing what color to use in a drawing allow children to assert their agency in a controlled environment. These choices help rebuild their sense of autonomy, which is crucial for trauma recovery. Beyond mere selection, allowing children to dictate the pace and direction of the therapy session can further enhance their feeling of control and support the therapeutic process by aligning it more closely with their intrinsic needs and comfort levels.

Symbolic play emerges as a powerful tool in trauma-informed therapy because it allows children to process traumatic experiences without confrontation, which can often be retraumatizing. The symbolic play uses metaphors and symbols instead of direct representations, which can provide emotional distance, making it safer for the child to engage with their feelings and memories. For example, a child who has experienced abandonment might use puppets to enact a scenario where a character gets lost but is safely returned home. This kind of play allows the child to explore the themes of loss and recovery at a comfortable remove and work through various outcomes, fostering a sense of resolution and healing. Choosing toys that encourage such expression—like dolls, animals, and figures that can represent different roles and scenarios—is essential in facilitating this therapeutic process.

Integrating relaxation techniques into play therapy can be incredibly beneficial in managing symptoms of trauma, such as anxiety, hypervigilance, and impulsivity. Techniques such as deep breathing, guided imagery, or progressive muscle relaxation can be woven into the play narrative. For instance, you might introduce a game where a character goes on a journey and encounters various challenges, using guided imagery to help the child visualize peaceful landscapes or safe places whenever the character feels scared or anxious. This makes the relaxation technique more engaging and relevant to the child and teaches them practical skills to calm themselves in stressful situations. These techniques provide practical coping mechanisms that children can carry into their everyday lives, enhancing their resilience and ability to manage emotional distress.

The thoughtful integration of these strategies within trauma-informed play therapy can transform a child's experience of trauma into a journey of healing. By prioritizing safety, choice, symbolic expression, and relaxation, you not only address the symptoms and behaviors associated with the trauma but also honor and support the child's overall emotional growth and recovery. This approach not only alleviates the impact of past trauma but also empowers the child with tools and insights that promote a healthier, more hopeful outlook on life.

2.4 Play Activities for Emotional Regulation: Helping Children Manage Their Feelings

Emotional regulation is a critical skill for children, aiding them in navigating the complexities of social interactions and personal feelings. Through play therapy, you can introduce fun and interactive ways to help children identify, express, and manage their emotions effectively. Emotion identification games are an excellent starting point. These games encourage children to recognize and name their feelings, a foundational step in emotional intelligence. Consider the game of emotion charades, where children act out different feelings while others guess the emotion. This makes learning about emotions fun and enhances children's ability to read and interpret emotional expressions, which is crucial for their social development. Another engaging activity is storytelling with emotional themes. Here, you might use story prompts that evoke various emotions, guiding the child to navigate the characters' feelings and reactions. This method helps children connect with and understand complex emotions in a narrative context, making it easier to relate these understandings to their experiences.

Problem-solving play

This activity is instrumental in teaching children how to manage emotional responses and develop resilience. Problem-solving requires children to think critically and make decisions, skills directly applicable to emotional regulation. For instance, engaging children in puzzle-solving activities where they encounter challenges or setbacks can teach them to manage frustration and think of alternative solutions. Similarly, building projects that require planning and adjustment can mimic real-life situations where things might not always go as planned. These activities provide a safe space for children to experience and cope with emotions like disappointment or frustration, encouraging them to develop persistence and a growth mindset.

Incorporating regulation tools during play sessions is another effective strategy to help children manage their emotions. Tools such as calm-down jars, where children watch the swirl of glitter settle, can be mesmerizing and soothing for moments of distress. Similarly, stress balls or fidget toys can provide a physical outlet for emotional energy, helping children calm down and regain focus. Introducing these tools during play therapy allows children to familiarize themselves with their benefits and learn how to use them independently when they experience emotional overwhelm.

Lastly, reflective listening is a powerful technique in play therapy that you can use to validate children's feelings and encourage the verbal expression of emotions. This involves listening attentively to the child, reflecting on what you hear without judgment, and asking open-ended questions to deepen understanding. For example, if a child expresses anger through play by knocking down a block tower, you might comment, "It seems like someone is feeling angry," followed by, "Can you tell me what got you so angry?" This approach validates the child's feelings and encourages them to explore these emotions in depth, providing a valuable skill set for emotional processing and communication.

Through these activities and techniques, play therapy becomes a dynamic tool for emotional education, equipping children with the skills necessary to navigate their emotional worlds effectively. Integrating these strategies into your sessions creates a nurturing environment where children can learn about and practice emotional regulation, fostering their development into emotionally intelligent individuals.

2.5 Sensory Play: Supporting Sensory Processing and Integration

Sensory play is a crucial bridge in connecting children with sensory processing challenges to the world around them, enhancing their ability to engage, focus, and ultimately derive joy and learning from their environment. For children who may find sensory integration overwhelming or need specific sensory inputs to remain engaged, sensory play provides a structured yet flexible approach to meeting these needs. Tactile activities, for example, are integral in sensory play. By engaging with materials like sand, water, or clay, children experience a range of textures that can stimulate or calm their sensory systems as needed. Sifting sand through fingers, manipulating squishy clay, or creating ripples in water not only delights the senses but also enhances fine motor skills and hand-eye coordination. These activities encourage children to explore properties such as texture, temperature, and resistance, which are essential components of sensory development. This form of play can be particularly therapeutic for children who may be hypersensitive to sensory inputs, as it allows them to engage with sensory stimuli in a controlled, predictable manner, gradually increasing their tolerance and comfort levels.

Balance and coordination games also serve as a cornerstone of sensory integration, especially for children struggling with proprioceptive or vestibular processing. Activities such as playing a bean bag toss or engaging in a game of hopscotch provide not just fun but also crucial challenges that promote body awareness and motor planning. For a child with sensory processing disorders, mastering the control needed to hop from one square to another or the coordination required to throw a bean bag accurately helps build confidence and competence in physical abilities. These games support the development of balance and coordination in a playful, engaging way, making the learning process enjoyable and rewarding. Additionally, they offer opportunities for social interaction and turn-taking, crucial skills for children who might otherwise find social engagement challenging.

Auditory sensory activities are tailored to aid children with auditory processing issues, helping them filter and make sense of the sounds in their environment. Engaging with musical instruments, for instance, allows children to explore sound hands-on, learning about volume, rhythm, and pitch in a setting where they can control the auditory input. Sound-matching games, where children match sounds to pictures or actions, can also enhance auditory discrimination skills. These activities support the development of auditory processing skills and integrate elements of memory and attention, which are often areas of difficulty for children with sensory processing challenges. By controlling the sound environment and making it an interactive, enjoyable part of play, children can gradually increase their ability to process auditory information more effectively, reducing feelings of being overwhelmed by noisy environments.

Visual-motor integration activities enhance the coordination between what a child sees and how they respond physically, an essential skill for academic tasks like writing and cutting with scissors. Drawing and tracing games are excellent methods for improving this integration. They allow children to practice following visual cues with motor responses, reinforcing neural pathways that make these processes more efficient. For a child struggling with visual motor integration, these activities provide a low-stress, high-engagement method of improving skills crucial for everyday tasks. Moreover, these games can be easily adapted to various skill levels. They can be made progressively more challenging as a child's abilities improve, ensuring they continue to be fun and beneficial.

Incorporating these diverse sensory play activities into therapy sessions or daily routines can significantly aid children with sensory processing challenges. By carefully selecting activities that address specific sensory needs, you create a supportive environment that fosters sensory development and overall cognitive and social growth. Through sensory play, children learn to navigate their sensory experiences more effectively, building a foundation for more complex learning and interaction in the future.

2.6 Inclusive Play Therapy: Adapting Activities for Diverse Abilities

In the vibrant realm of play therapy, embracing the diversity of children's abilities enriches the therapeutic experience and broadens the impact of our interventions. Universal design in play therapy isn't just an approach but a commitment to creating an environment where activities are accessible and enjoyable for children of all abilities. This concept involves designing play sessions and choosing materials catering to a wide range of physical, cognitive, and emotional needs without substantial adaptation. For instance, incorporating wide pathways between play stations accommodates children with mobility aids, while sensory-friendly zones can offer respite for those with sensory sensitivities. The key is to embed flexibility and adaptability into the core design of play activities, ensuring every child can participate meaningfully without feeling sidelined.

The evolution of play therapy includes integrating adaptive play equipment, which plays a pivotal role in leveling the playing field for children with varying abilities. Adaptive play equipment ranges from modified board games with more extensive, easy-to-handle pieces for children with motor difficulties to digital apps that can be operated with touch or eye movements, catering to children with limited mobility. Furthermore, assistive technology like voice-to-text software or augmentative communication devices can be seamlessly integrated into play scenarios, enabling children who face challenges with verbal communication to participate fully and express themselves on par with their peers. These adaptations enhance participation and foster an inclusive atmosphere where differences are acknowledged and accommodated with creativity and respect.

Collaborative play strategies are another cornerstone of inclusive play therapy. Techniques such as buddy systems or peer-assisted play encourage children of different abilities to work together towards common goals. In a buddy system, a child with advanced social skills might be paired with a peer who finds social interaction challenging. This pairing can help the latter learn through modeling and direct interaction, all within the naturalistic play setting. Peer-assisted play promotes social skills and nurtures empathy and understanding among children as they learn to recognize and appreciate each other's strengths and challenges. The beauty of these collaborative strategies lies in their dual benefit. While they support the developmental needs of children with specific challenges, they also cultivate an environment of cooperation and mutual respect, which are crucial values for all participants.

Cultural adaptations in play activities ensure that the therapy is not only inclusive in terms of abilities but also respectful and reflective of the children's diverse cultural backgrounds. This involves more than just including culturally diverse toys and materials; it extends to adapting scenarios and play narratives that resonate with the children's cultural experiences and family backgrounds. For example, incorporating stories or games that are part of a child's cultural heritage can provide comfort and familiarity, enhancing their engagement and connection to the therapy. Additionally, being mindful of cultural norms and values related to play, communication styles, and social interactions can guide therapists in crafting culturally sensitive and appropriately challenging sessions.

In implementing these inclusive strategies, play therapy transcends traditional boundaries, offering a dynamic and flexible approach that respects and celebrates the diversity of all children. By ensuring that our therapeutic practices are inclusive, we not only advocate for equality and accessibility but also enrich the therapeutic experience, making it more effective and transformative for everyone involved.

As we conclude this exploration of inclusive play therapy, remember that the essence of our work lies in recognizing each child's unique abilities and creating opportunities for them to thrive. The strategies discussed here—from universal design to collaborative play—are techniques and reflections of our commitment to honor and elevate every child's potential. As you move forward, let these principles guide you in crafting therapeutic experiences as diverse and vibrant as the children you serve, setting a solid foundation for future chapters.

Chapter 3

Strengthening Bonds Through Play

In the tapestry of childhood development, the threads of emotional bonds between caregivers and children are woven with vibrant colors of trust, understanding, and mutual respect. Play, in its most nurturing form, guides these threads as a gentle hand, strengthening the fabric that connects the hearts of children and adults alike. This chapter delves into attachment-based play activities, where each playful interaction entertains and deepens the bonds forming a child's sense of security and belonging.

3.1 Attachment-Based Play Activities: Strengthening the Caregiver-Child Bond

Introduction to Attachment-Based Play

Attachment-based play is a strategic approach within play therapy that focuses on strengthening the emotional and psychological bonds between a child and their caregiver. Rooted in attachment theory, which emphasizes the importance of healthy early relationships for optimal development, this play is tailored to enhance empathy, trust, and understanding. Through structured play activities that promote close interaction, caregivers are not just participants in a child's world of imagination but become co-architects of their emotional landscape, building bridges of connectivity beyond the playroom.

Mirroring Activities

One of the most effective techniques in attachment-based play is mirroring activities. Here, caregivers reflect a child's actions or emotions during play, acting as a mirror that validates and acknowledges the child's feelings and perspectives. For instance, if a child pretends to be a chef preparing a meal, the caregiver might also prepare an imaginary dish, following the child's lead. This activity does more than mimic; it shows the child that their thoughts and activities are essential and worthy of attention. Emotionally, when a child displays signs of sadness or happiness in their play, mirroring these emotions by expressing similar feelings can enhance their emotional vocabulary and empathy, promoting a deeper connection between the caregiver and the child.

Joint Creative Projects

Collaborative projects like building a model or creating a piece of art are central to attachment-based play. These activities require cooperation and shared decision-making, fostering teamwork and enhancing emotional bonds through a shared sense of accomplishment. For example, constructing a birdhouse requires planning, sharing tasks, and problem-solving, encouraging dialogue and patience. As the project progresses, the child and caregiver build a physical structure and a tower of mutual respect and understanding, cementing their bond over shared goals and achievements.

Routine Play Sessions

Establishing regular, scheduled play sessions is another pillar of attachment-based play. Consistency is vital in fostering a secure environment; knowing that there are dedicated times for interactions builds anticipation and trust. These routine playtimes become sacred, reliable moments of connection in a child's often chaotic world, providing them with stability and a rhythm of engagement that reinforces their sense of security and attachment. Whether it's a nightly bedtime story or a weekly game night, the predictability of these interactions embeds a deep understanding of security and belonging in the child, essential components of a robust and healthy relationship.

Interactive Element: Reflection Sessions

Consider incorporating a weekly reflection session at the end of each play activity where you and the child can discuss what was most enjoyable or challenging about the experience. This encourages verbal expression of thoughts and feelings and enhances mutual understanding, providing valuable insights into each other's emotional worlds. This practice can transform simple play activities into profound emotional growth and bonding opportunities.

In the dance of attachment-based play, each step, each shared smile, and every joint venture is a thread pulling the hearts of caregivers and children closer. As we weave through the play's fabric, the bonds fortified in these moments lay the groundwork for the emotional resilience and interpersonal skills children carry into their future. This chapter, a mosaic of strategies and heartfelt interactions, offers you the tools to participate in and enrich this beautiful dance, strengthening the bonds that make growing up a shared, joyous adventure.

3.2 Play Therapies for Parent Involvement: Techniques for Families

Each member plays a unique role in the dynamic interplay of family life, contributing to the shared tapestry of experiences and emotions. Play therapy, when extended to include all family members, becomes a powerful conduit for enhancing communication, understanding, and joy within the family unit. Encouraging the establishment of family play nights is one such initiative where every family member—from the youngest child to the elders—comes together to engage in activities designed to celebrate inclusivity and collective enjoyment. Imagine setting aside one evening each week where the family gathers, not around the television, but around a game board or a craft project. These nights are not just about having fun; they are about creating a space where family members can share experiences, learn about each other's day, and jointly solve problems presented by the game or activity. The choice of activities on these nights should cater to all ages and interests, ensuring that each family member feels included and valued. This could range from interactive board games that provoke thought and strategy to creative arts and crafts that express individuality and foster a sense of accomplishment when displayed at home.

The role of parents in facilitating therapeutic play is pivotal, and as such, offering guidelines for training parents in therapeutic play techniques is essential. This training empowers parents to conduct meaningful play sessions independently, reinforcing the skills learned during formal therapy sessions and integrating them into the child's everyday environment. This training might include workshops where parents know the basics of play therapy under the guidance of a professional, focusing on understanding the objectives of different play activities and how to tailor them to meet their child's specific emotional or developmental needs. For instance, parents can learn how to use puppet play to help a child express difficult emotion or how to set up a role-play session that allows a child to explore various solutions to a problem. By equipping parents with these skills, play therapy becomes a more consistent and integral part of the child's life, providing ongoing support and reinforcing therapeutic goals.

Role-reversal play is another fascinating aspect of family-oriented play therapy. In these scenarios, children and parents switch roles, which can be an eye-opening experience for both. For example, in a role-reversal play session, a parent might take on the role of the child, having to follow the rules set by the child playing the 'parent.' This reversal can give parents insight into how their child perceives adult reactions and decisions while children get a taste of the responsibilities and challenges parents face. This mutual empathy fostered through role reversal can bridge gaps in understanding and improve family dynamics, making it easier for family members to appreciate and empathize with each other's roles and efforts within the family.

Incorporating guided dialogue into play is crucial in helping family members express feelings and resolve conflicts in a supportive environment. This method involves structuring play sessions that encourage open communication and reflection. For instance, a parent might initiate a discussion after a family game by asking each member what they felt about the game, what they learned, and if anything during the play made them feel uncomfortable or happy. These guided dialogues help identify underlying issues that might not surface in regular conversations, providing a safe space to explore solutions. The therapist can train parents to use these dialogues effectively during play, ensuring that conversations remain positive and constructive, focusing on understanding and addressing feelings and behaviors rather than assigning blame.

Engaging families in play therapy through these innovative and inclusive methods enhances the child's therapeutic outcomes. It strengthens the family unit, making it more resilient to the challenges of everyday life. By fostering open communication, mutual understanding, and collective enjoyment, play therapy can transform family dynamics, enriching the lives of all family members and creating a harmonious home environment where every member feels understood, appreciated, and integral to the family's well-being.

3.3 Building Trust Through Play: Activities That Foster Security and Reliability

In the constellation of relationships that form around a young child, trust is the shining star that guides their interactions and shapes their perception of the world. In play therapy, we find a unique opportunity to cultivate and reinforce this trust through carefully structured activities that delight and teach profound, enduring lessons about reliability and mutual respect. Trust-building games, essential components of this therapeutic toolkit, are designed to create experiences where trust is practiced and experienced viscerally, leaving a lasting imprint on young minds.

Consider trust falls or blindfolded guidance activities—games that, by their very nature, require a leap of faith. In a trust fall, a child allows themselves to fall backward, relying on another person to catch them. This simple act is profound in its implications; it teaches the child that they can depend on others and that their vulnerability will not be exploited but supported. Blindfolded guidance games, where one child guides another who cannot see, deepen communication and foster a bond where guiding and being guided become acts of mutual reliance and care. Each of these games serves a dual purpose: they are inherently fun and engaging, which encourages participation, but they also establish a framework where trust is repeatedly tested and proven, building a solid foundation of reliability between participants.

The consistency of rules in play is another vital element in fostering trust. When rules are applied fairly and predictably, and caregivers model this consistency, children learn that the world operates within understandable and reliable boundaries. Fair play becomes a microcosm of broader social interactions, teaching children that they can expect consistency in how others treat them and how they should treat others. For instance, when a game's rules are upheld consistently, a child learns that no individual is above the rules, reinforcing concepts of fairness and justice. Caregivers can further enhance this learning by explicitly discussing the importance of fair play and being transparent about the reasons behind specific rules. This helps children understand and respect these boundaries, seeing them as protective rather than restrictive.

Secret Keeper activities introduce an intriguing dimension to play therapy by nurturing private bonding through sharing secrets or confidential information. These activities might involve a game where a child is told a 'secret' about the story's character, which they are then asked to keep safe or solve within the play narrative. This makes the play more engaging by adding a layer of intrigue and elevates the child's sense of responsibility and trustworthiness. It's a playful yet potent reminder that they are trusted with important information, reinforcing their self-esteem and respect for confidentiality. As children engage in these activities, they learn the value of discretion and the trust others place in them, which informs how they handle real-life confidences.

Reward-based systems within play, when used judiciously, can significantly reinforce positive interactions and trustworthy behavior. It is crucial, however, that these rewards are consistent and fair, mirroring the reliability we hope to instill in the children themselves. For example, a system where children earn points for demonstrating trustworthiness and reliability can be highly effective. Points might be awarded for acts such as keeping promises, playing fairly, or helping others during play. These points could be exchanged for rewards, such as choosing a game or a small prize. The key is ensuring that the link between trustworthy behavior and rewards is clear and consistent so children understand and internalize the value of reliability and reliability. This system motivates children to adhere to the behaviors taught, making learning enjoyable and rewarding.

Incorporating these activities into play therapy offers a dynamic approach to building trust among children. By engaging them in games that require trust, ensuring consistency in the application of rules, involving them in secret-keeping games, and rewarding trustworthy behaviors, we lay down stepping stones towards nurturing individuals who value and embody reliability and trust in their interactions. As you continue to guide children through these activities, remember that each game, each rule, and each secret kept is a thread weaving a stronger bond of trust, not just between the child and their peers but with the broader world they are growing into.

3.4 Fun and Engaging Co-Play: Games and Activities for Parents and Children

In the lively arena of family activities, the shared joy and learning that emerge from interactive board games are unparalleled. These games are not just about fun; they are a fertile ground for cultivating skills like communication and problem-solving within a family setting. Imagine sitting around a table where each family member, young and old, is engaged in a game that requires both luck, strategic thinking, and collaboration, games such as "Ticket to Ride" or "Catan," where players build routes or gather resources, necessitate planning and negotiation, skills valuable both on and off the game board. These games encourage players to articulate their strategies and negotiate with others, fostering communication skills and teaching the value of planning and compromise. Moreover, the cooperative board game "Pandemic" requires players to work together to stop global outbreaks, which can be a thrilling way for families to experience teamwork and collective problem-solving in action. Through these interactive board games, families can experience the joy of play, intertwined with the growth of personal and interpersonal skills, strengthening family bonds in laughter and learning.

Moving beyond the board, physical play activities such as sports or obstacle courses offer a dynamic way to enhance family connections while promoting health and physical fitness. Engaging in a family soccer match or setting up a backyard obstacle course can be an exhilarating afternoon. These activities require cooperation and physical support as family members cheer each other on and navigate challenges together. For instance, creating a simple obstacle course with stations like a hula hoop hop, a crawl under a rope, and a balance beam provides physical challenges and opportunities for encouraging each other through physical and verbal support. Such activities keep the body active and strengthen emotional bonds through shared experiences and achievements. They transform a mundane afternoon into an adventure where each family member can contribute, learn, and grow individually and as part of a team.

In today's digital age, incorporating technology into family playtime can also offer unique opportunities for bonding and learning. While moderation is vital, judicious use of technology can unite families and provide common ground for enjoyment and education. Engaging with apps or video games that are designed for multiple players can turn screen time into an interactive family experience. Games like "Minecraft" can be played cooperatively and offer a platform for creativity and problem-solving as family members build and explore virtual worlds together. Apps incorporating learning elements, like those for solving puzzles or learning about geography, can also be excellent for families, making learning fun and accessible. It's essential, however, to select apps and games that encourage interaction rather than solitary play, ensuring that technology acts as a bridge, rather than a barrier, in family connections.

Creative storytelling is another enriching activity that can enhance family dynamics by fostering creativity, listening skills, and shared narrative development. This can involve one family member starting a story and others adding to it or each person creating a character and collectively advancing the plot. This form of play allows children and adults to step into different roles and perspectives, sparking imagination and empathy. Moreover, building on each other's ideas can reinforce the values of respect and listening, as each narrative contribution is valued and built upon. Storytelling can transport a family to another world created and shared by them, strengthening their bond through the magic of narrative.

Families engaging in these diverse play activities weave a more decadent, more connected relationship fabric. Each game, each story, and each physical challenge becomes a chapter in their shared family story, filled with learning, laughter, and love. Through these playful interactions, families build memories and develop a deeper understanding and appreciation of each other, laying a solid foundation for lifelong relationships.

3.5 The Role of Play in Family Therapy: Bringing Families Together

In family therapy, integrating play into the therapeutic process is not merely about adding a layer of fun or engagement; it's about tapping into play's profound ability to mirror and reshape family dynamics. Various models of family therapy utilize play to deepen emotional connections and facilitate healing. One such model is filial therapy, which empowers parents to participate actively in their child's therapeutic play sessions. Under the guidance of a therapist, parents learn specific play skills that they then use during supervised 'play times' with their child. This approach does more than address the child's issues—it enhances the parent-child relationship, fostering understanding and empathy through the shared language of play. The benefits of such models are manifold. They help mitigate the child's behavioral or emotional issues and equip parents with practical communication tools, enhancing their ability to provide ongoing emotional support. The methodology, centered around structured training sessions for parents followed by supervised interactive play, ensures that the therapeutic goals are met while strengthening the familial bonds.

Play's utility extends beyond just facilitating bonding—it serves as a dynamic lens through which therapists can observe and modify family dynamics. In a typical family play session, therapists might introduce specific games that require various family members to collaborate, compete, or communicate in structured ways. These play scenarios can reveal underlying relational patterns, power dynamics, and conflict styles within the family unit, offering invaluable insights to the therapist. For example, a game that requires family members to build a structure together might bring out latent issues of control or cooperation, reflecting broader familial interactions. The therapist can then guide the family to reflect on these dynamics and explore healthier ways to interact. These insights are pivotal as they provide a real-time, contextual understanding of the family's interpersonal relationships. They allow for targeted interventions that address the root causes of familial conflicts or challenges.

Addressing conflicts within the family context requires more than conversation; it needs a medium where everyone can engage emotionally and cognitively. Play-based conflict resolution strategy uses play to help family members express, process, and resolve conflicts. By creating a play scenario that metaphorically represents a family conflict, therapists can guide family members through identifying the conflict, expressing their feelings about it, and working together to find a resolution. For instance, using a board game that involves resource allocation, family members might naturally begin to discuss issues of fairness or need, which can then be gently guided to reflect real-life conflicts about sharing household responsibilities or attention. Play's safe and somewhat abstract context allows emotions and thoughts to surface less threateningly, promoting understanding and empathy among family members.

Moreover, cultural considerations are crucial in ensuring family therapy is respectful and relevant to all family members. A family's cultural background can significantly influence their values, communication styles, and relationship dynamics. When integrating play into family therapy, choosing play activities and materials that are culturally respectful and relevant is vital. For instance, integrating narrative-based play can be particularly effective for families from backgrounds where storytelling is a central tradition. Similarly, understanding cultural nuances related to gender roles or authority figures can help select play activities that do not inadvertently conflict with a family's cultural values. This cultural sensitivity ensures that the therapy is effective and helps build trust and respect between the therapist and the family members, fostering a therapeutic environment that honors each individual's identity and background.

In this exploration of the role of play in family therapy, we uncover the multifaceted ways in which play can heal, reveal, and enrich family interactions. From structured models like filial therapy to dynamic play-based conflict resolution techniques, play-in family therapy provides a unique and powerful tool for therapists to foster deeper understanding and more effective communication within families. As these methods continue to evolve and adapt, they promise to transform family therapy into a more engaging, insightful, and empathetic process, where every game played, and every role assumed can lead to meaningful moments of connection and growth.

3.6 Addressing Parental Concerns: Effective Communication Through Play

Navigating the intricate landscape of a child's learning and development presents a unique set of challenges and concerns for parents. Educational play emerges as a strategic bridge, melding the joy of play with the rigor of learning, creating an environment where children thrive emotionally and academically. By weaving educational goals seamlessly into the fabric of play, parents can address their concerns about academic readiness and intellectual growth without sacrificing the fun and spontaneity that play naturally brings. Consider integrating counting games, alphabet puzzles, or science-themed activities that align with educational standards yet are delivered through playful engagement. These activities can be as simple as counting blocks to build a tower, which subtly teaches basic mathematics, or as intricate as setting up a backyard habitat to explore biology. Each game is designed to educate and spark curiosity and joy, making learning a vibrant part of children's playtime. This approach helps children associate learning with positive experiences, fostering a lifelong love for education.

Addressing behavioral issues through play offers a dynamic and empathetic way for parents to guide their children toward appropriate behaviors and social skills. Play-based techniques provide a non-threatening avenue to explore the consequences of actions and learn alternative behaviors. Games that require turn-taking, sharing, or cooperating can be particularly beneficial. For instance, a board game that requires players to collaborate to achieve a common goal teaches the value of working together while highlighting the social rewards of shared success. Role-playing various social situations can also help children understand and practice appropriate responses; for example, role-playing a situation where one has to apologize or share toys can reinforce these behaviors in a fun, engaging way. Children learn essential social rules and behaviors critical to their immediate environment and broader society through these playful interactions.

Emotional expression through play is another cornerstone of effective communication between parents and children. Activities such as puppet shows or creative arts provide a safe outlet for children to express complex or challenging emotions. Children can project their feelings onto the characters in a puppet show, allowing them to deal with emotions indirectly, which can be less intimidating and more manageable. Art activities like drawing or sculpting can similarly offer children a way to manifest their feelings physically, providing parents with a visual and tangible way to understand their child's emotional world. These activities allow children to express their emotions in a controlled, therapeutic setting and give parents insight into the feelings their child may be unable to verbalize, enhancing empathy and understanding within the family.

Parental guidance and support in using play to communicate about sensitive topics are crucial in fostering an open and trusting family environment. Structuring conversations within the context of play can make discussing sensitive topics less daunting for both parent and child. Parents can use story-based games to introduce scenarios that mirror real-life issues, guiding the child through the problem-solving process in an age-appropriate and empathetic way. For example, a board game involving peer pressure scenarios can serve as a springboard for discussions about making choices and standing up for oneself. Ensuring these conversations are at the right developmental level is critical, as it respects the child's cognitive and emotional capacities, making the discussion more effective and meaningful. By integrating these strategies into play, parents can address sensitive issues in a manner that children understand and respond to, fostering effective communication and emotional closeness.

Educational play, behavioral guidance, emotional expression, and sensitive communication address parental concerns effectively while fostering a nurturing environment where children feel understood and supported. As these elements combine within the playful interactions between parent and child, they form a robust framework for addressing parents' concerns regarding their child's growth and development. Through this approach, play becomes more than just a simple activity; it becomes a vital tool in developing healthy, well-rounded individuals equipped to face the world's challenges with confidence and resilience.

In wrapping up this exploration into the intersection of play and parental guidance, we reaffirm the transformative power of play in addressing specific developmental concerns and strengthening the bonds of understanding and communication within the family. As we transition into the next chapter, we carry forward the insights and strategies that make play a profound agent of growth and connection, ready to explore new dimensions and applications in the ever-evolving narrative of child development.

Chapter 4

Digital Well-Being in the Play Therapy Space

Managing our children's engagement with technology becomes crucial in an era where digital landscapes often intersect with our physical realities. The glow of screens, though illuminating, carries the potential to overshadow the rich experiences offered by the offline world. As we navigate this chapter, we will explore how play-based strategies can mitigate the effects of excessive screen time and enhance children's overall well-being. Here, you'll discover methods to weave the digital with the tangible in a balanced tapestry that supports healthy development.

4.1 Managing Screen Time: Play-Based Strategies to Reduce Digital Dependence

The digital age brings many benefits, from access to a world of information to instant connectivity with others. However, the impact of excessive screen time on children can be profound, affecting their social skills, emotional well-being, and cognitive development. Children immersed in screens may miss critical interpersonal interactions and physical activities essential for holistic growth. This section introduces structured play interventions designed to attract children away from screens, engaging them in the tangible joys of the world around them.

Scheduled play interventions form the cornerstone of our strategy to reduce screen dependency. By organizing play sessions that are both structured and timed, children can enjoy a balanced routine that includes periods of digital use and periods without. For instance, establish a schedule where screen time is allowed for 30 minutes after school, followed by an hour of monitored, structured play that involves physical activity or creative arts. Using timers and visual cues helps children understand and adhere to these boundaries. Visual cues, such as a colorful clock or a timer app, can signal when screen time is about to end, preparing them for the transition. This method reduces screen time and enhances children's focus on activities, promoting cognitive and physical skills.

Implementing a system of playful rewards for reduced screen time can further encourage children to engage in non-digital activities. For example, a points system can be introduced where children earn points for every hour spent off-screen. These points could be exchanged for rewards such as a weekend activity or a small toy. This system motivates children to reduce screen usage and makes the process engaging. It teaches them the value of earning through positive behavior, instilling a sense of accomplishment and responsibility.

Educational role plays are a dynamic tool to illustrate the effects of excessive screen time and the benefits of diversified activities. In these role-playing sessions, children might enact scenarios where one character spends too much time on screens and faces various consequences, such as feeling tired or having a headache. In contrast, another character engages in different activities and displays more energy and happiness. These role plays can be powerful as they allow children to visually and emotionally process the impacts of their choices regarding screen use. By actively participating in these stories, children can better understand the tangible benefits of balanced habits and are more likely to internalize these lessons.

Interactive Element: Reflection Section

Take a moment to reflect on your family's current screen time habits. Consider what changes might be beneficial and how you might use play to facilitate these changes. This reflection can be a starting point for implementing the strategies discussed, tailored to fit your unique family dynamics.

In weaving these strategies into the fabric of daily routines, the goal is to reduce screen time and enrich children's lives with experiences that foster their social, emotional, and cognitive development. As we continue to explore the integration of digital and physical play, these foundational practices set the stage for a balanced approach that honors the benefits of technology while promoting a healthy, engaging, and active lifestyle.

4.2 Digital and Physical Play Balance: Creating Healthy Media Habits

In today's fast-paced digital world, striking a harmonious balance between screen time and physical play is more crucial than ever for children's holistic development. The allure of digital devices is undeniable; they captivate with interactive experiences and instant connectivity. However, integrating these digital experiences with physical play can foster a richer developmental landscape for children—where cognitive, social, and physical growth occurs seamlessly across digital and tangible realms.

One effective strategy to cultivate such a balance involves alternating tech days with tech-free days. This approach regulates screen time and encourages children to engage deeply with the physical world. Activities like nature hikes, craft sessions, or sports can take center stage on tech-free days, offering diverse experiences that stimulate physical activity and creativity. Conversely, tech days can be structured to include educational apps and games that complement the learning themes explored during tech-free periods. For instance, after a day of learning about plants outdoors, children might engage with a botany app that reinforces their learning through interactive quizzes or virtual garden-building activities. This alternation prevents the overuse of digital devices and enriches the child's learning experience, making transitions between digital and non-digital play natural and productive.

Integrative play activities that blend digital and physical elements can also significantly enhance this balanced approach. Using technology to create real-world treasure hunts is a splendid example. Apps that overlay digital clues onto physical locations encourage children to navigate the real world using digital cues, merging screen time with physical activity. This augmented reality game compels children to run, think, and observe their environment closely, effectively marrying digital games' cognitive engagement with outdoor play's physical exertion.

Similarly, incorporating digital storytelling elements into a physical play, like a puppet show, can transform a traditional activity into an interactive multimedia experience. For example, children can use a simple video recording app to create special effects for a live puppet show, enhancing their storytelling with digital enhancements that complement the physical performance.

Parental involvement is pivotal in setting and enforcing boundaries for digital play. It's essential for parents to actively participate in both digital and physical play activities to model and monitor appropriate media habits. Co-playing video games offer a chance to monitor the content, ensure it's age-appropriate, and discuss the game's themes, challenges, and what's being learned. This active involvement helps parents guide their children in understanding and critiquing digital content, making them more mindful of their screen time activities. Moreover, by joining in physical play, parents reinforce the value of non-digital engagement, showing that fun and learning don't solely reside within digital devices. These shared activities strengthen familial bonds and ensure parents are seen as partners in play, not just supervisors.

The role of caregivers in modeling balanced media habits cannot be overstated. Children often emulate adult behaviors, and caregivers who visibly moderate their screen use, dedicating time to unplugged activities, set a powerful example. Caregivers can further this by being fully present during playtimes—putting aside their devices to focus on shared activities, whether building a puzzle or playing a game of catch. This shows children the value placed on direct interaction and physical play and establishes a family culture where digital devices are tools, not focal points of daily life. By embodying these habits, caregivers clearly communicate the importance of balance and the value of diverse digital or physical experiences.

These strategies make achieving a healthy balance goal between digital and physical play attainable. By weaving together the benefits of both worlds, we can support children in developing a rounded set of skills and habits that will serve them well in an increasingly digital future while still grounding them in the rich, irreplaceable experiences of the physical world. As we progress through this digital age, let us remain committed to nurturing these balanced habits, ensuring our young ones grow as capable navigators of both the virtual and the tangible landscapes they inhabit.

4.3 Tech-Free Play Therapy: Engaging Alternatives to Screen-Based Activities

In the vibrant landscape of child development, reintroducing traditional play activities serves as a refreshing counterbalance to the digital-heavy tendencies of modern entertainment. These activities, encompassing board games, crafts, and outdoor sports, do more than merely entertain; they foster many developmental benefits, including strategic thinking, fine motor skills, and physical health. Consider the timeless appeal of board games like chess or checkers, which captivate children's strategic thinking and enhance their ability to anticipate consequences and plan. Similarly, crafts such as painting, knitting, or model building engage children's fine motor skills and creativity, offering them a sense of accomplishment and the joy of creating something tangible. Outdoor sports, from soccer to tag, provide essential physical activity and teach teamwork and resilience in ways that digital games cannot replicate. These activities function collectively as entertainment and crucial building blocks in a child's growth, promoting cognitive and physical development and emotional well-being.

Therapeutic art projects specialize in tech-free play therapy, providing a dual benefit of creativity and emotional expression. Art, in its myriad forms, offers children a non-verbal mode of communication that can be particularly therapeutic. For instance, clay modeling sessions can help children channel their inner thoughts and emotions into creating something concrete, which can be incredibly satisfying and enlightening. Another project might involve making a 'mood collage,' where children choose colors, pictures, and textures that reflect their feelings, helping them to articulate complex emotions through visual media. These art projects not only divert focus from screens but also profoundly engage children's attention, drawing them into a meditative state of flow that screens rarely achieve. By integrating these projects into regular therapy sessions, children can explore and express their emotions in a supportive environment, fostering emotional healing and self-expression.

Interactive storytelling is another enriching, tech-free activity where children become co-creators of narratives, using their imagination, costumes, and props. Unlike passive consumption of stories through screens, interactive storytelling involves children actively; they might assume the roles of characters, influence the plot, or even create dialogue on the spot. This form of storytelling makes the narrative experience immersive and deeply personal. Children not only hear or see a story—they live it. The use of costumes and props enhances this experience, making the story tangible and real. This involvement can profoundly empower children as they see their ideas and voices shaping the story's direction, which can be particularly therapeutic for those who may feel unheard or powerless in their everyday lives.

Sensory bins and tactile play setups present a universe of exploration for children, where they can indulge their senses without the mediation of a screen. These setups typically involve containers filled with sand, water, beans, or rice, which children can dig into, pour, or sift through. These simple activities are surprisingly robust in calming children's minds and keeping their hands engaged. For children who experience sensory processing issues, these bins can be customized to provide the exact level of sensory input they need to feel calm and focused. Adding elements like scented oils, smooth pebbles, or squishy toys can enhance the sensory experience, making it both therapeutic and deeply satisfying. Engaging with these materials provides sensory feedback that digital devices cannot offer, promoting sensory integration skills and offering children a soothing, grounding experience.

In embracing these tech-free play therapy activities, the goal is to enrich the therapeutic landscape with diverse, engaging, and developmentally beneficial experiences. Each activity has advantages, from enhancing cognitive abilities and fine motor skills to fostering emotional expression and sensory integration. By offering children these varied and enriching experiences, we help them develop essential life skills and joyful, memorable experiences that profoundly shape their growth.

4.4 Using Technology Responsibly in Play Therapy: When Tech Enhances Growth

In the intricate dance of integrating technology into play therapy, the goal is not merely to incorporate digital tools for their own sake but to enhance and support therapeutic objectives meaningfully. Selective tech integration allows us to harness the precise benefits of digital advancements while maintaining the therapeutic essence of play. Consider, for instance, mood-tracking apps or virtual reality (VR) setups that can dramatically transform therapeutic outcomes. Mood tracking apps, when used responsibly under the guidance of a therapist, can provide insightful data on a child's emotional patterns, offering a concrete basis for discussions and interventions. This real-time emotional logging helps the therapist and child identify triggers and trends in emotional responses, fostering a more tailored therapeutic approach. VR, on the other hand, opens up a world of possibilities for phobia management. By creating controlled, immersive environments, children can confront and work through their fears in a safe setting, gradually reducing their anxiety through guided exposure and therapeutic techniques. The key to successful tech integration is its purposeful use—ensuring that each digital tool directly contributes to the therapy's aims, enhancing the therapeutic journey rather than distracting from it.

In navigating the landscape of digital tools in play therapy, it's imperative to establish clear guidelines on the types of technology appropriate for different therapeutic needs. This consideration ensures that the technology used is adequate and proper for the child's age, cognitive level, and specific therapeutic goals. For instance, interactive story apps might be suitable for a child who needs help with narrative skills or understanding sequences of events. At the same time, simple cause-and-effect games might be better suited for a child working on motor skills or cause-and-effect reasoning. Each digital tool should be chosen with a clear rationale, and its use should be monitored to ensure it aligns with the intended therapeutic outcomes. Moderation is crucial; digital tools should complement, not replace, traditional play therapy techniques. They should be balanced, ensuring children still benefit from conventional play's rich, tactile, and interpersonal experiences.

Turning our focus to digital tools that promote creativity, drawing tablets or music creation apps present exciting opportunities. These tools can be integrated into play therapy by enabling children to express themselves artistically in ways that might be less accessible through traditional mediums. A drawing tablet, for example, can allow a child to experiment with different artistic styles without the limitations of physical media, providing an unlimited canvas and many options for colors and effects. This can be remarkably freeing for children who may feel inhibited by the permanence of paint or crayons. Similarly, music creation apps can enable children to compose and manipulate sounds, which can be therapeutically beneficial and deeply satisfying. These creative expressions enhance children's engagement and enjoyment and provide valuable insights into their feelings and thoughts, facilitating deeper therapeutic exploration.

Lastly, evaluating the effectiveness and appropriateness of digital tools is fundamental to responsible technology use in play therapy. This evaluation should consider several factors, including the tool's educational and therapeutic value, user-friendliness, and privacy concerns. For example, an app that complies with privacy regulations such as COPPA (Children's Online Privacy Protection Act) ensures that children's data is protected. Furthermore, the therapeutic value of the app should be assessed based on evidence-based criteria, such as whether it has been tested in similar therapeutic settings and what measurable outcomes it supports. Feedback from children and their caregivers can also provide practical insights into the tool's effectiveness and engagement level, helping therapists make informed decisions about continuing or modifying its use. This ongoing evaluation ensures that the digital tools used remain relevant and beneficial and safeguards the integrity of the therapeutic process, maintaining a focus on the child's well-being and growth.

4.5 Activities for Digital Detox: Promoting Offline Interactions

In the digital age, fostering genuine, screen-free interactions is becoming increasingly vital, not just for children but for families as a whole. The concept of a digital detox— intentionally setting aside time to disconnect from electronic devices—offers a refreshing opportunity to engage in the physical world with mindfulness and presence. To support this, creating digital detox challenges can be a transformative initiative. These challenges, structured as fun, engaging activities with clear goals, encourage children and their families to enjoy time together without the constant interruption of screens. Imagine a weekend challenge where each family member pledges to go screen-free for 24 hours while participating in pre-planned activities such as a picnic in the park, a family art project, or a storytelling session. This structured approach sets clear expectations and fills the time with enriching experiences that provide meaningful alternatives to digital engagement.

The benefits of these detox challenges extend beyond just reducing screen time—they enhance familial bonds, improve social skills, and encourage creative and physical activities that contribute to overall health. Moreover, they teach children self-regulation and the value of experiencing the world directly, not just through digital media. Encouraging families to plan these detox periods together also ensures that everyone is invested and that the activities are enjoyable and anticipated. This makes the digital detox something to look forward to rather than a chore.

Extending beyond individual and family challenges, organizing group play activities that require no digital devices is another robust strategy to promote enriched social interactions. Activities like team sports, drama clubs, or craft groups provide dynamic social settings where children can develop interpersonal skills such as communication, teamwork, and empathy. For example, joining a local soccer team or a drama club keeps children physically active and creatively engaged. It embeds them in a community with shared interests, where social bonds can flourish outside the digital realm. These activities provide a platform for children to express themselves, confront challenges, and celebrate successes in real-time with their peers, as well as critical aspects of their social and emotional development.

Incorporating mindfulness and meditation into play sessions is another effective method to enhance focus and counterbalance the overstimulation often associated with excessive screen use. Simple mindfulness exercises, like deep breathing games or yoga stretches, can be integrated into playtime, teaching children how to calm their minds and bodies. These practices can be beneficial during transitions from high-energy activities to quieter, more focused play, helping children regain their center after excitement or frustration. Additionally, meditation can be introduced through guided imagery where children imagine a peaceful scene, perhaps a quiet forest or a calm beach, which can help them learn to manage anxiety and stress. These mindfulness practices foster a sense of inner peace and presence, qualities that are often overshadowed in the fast-paced digital world.

Implementing a reward system for engaging in offline interactions can further reinforce the benefits of face-to-face play and communication. Rewards for interaction might include earning points for every hour spent playing outside, which could be exchanged for a special privilege, such as choosing a family movie to watch or selecting a new board game. This system motivates children to engage more in offline activities and makes these activities more appealing and rewarding. However, these rewards must be consistent with the spirit of digital detox; instead, they should enhance the child's appreciation for and engagement with the offline world.

These strategies collectively create a multifaceted approach to digital detox, weaving together challenges, group activities, mindfulness practices, and incentives to foster healthier, more engaged, and more mindful interactions in the physical world. By embracing these approaches, you encourage children to discover and relish the joys and benefits of life beyond screens, nurturing their ability to connect with themselves and others in more meaningful ways.

4.6 Evaluating Digital Play Tools: What to Use and What to Avoid

In the ever-evolving landscape of digital tools available for play therapy, making informed selections that align closely with therapeutic goals, safeguard user safety, and provide substantial educational value is crucial. Establishing clear criteria for selecting these tools is the first step in ensuring that technology integration into play therapy remains innovative but also appropriate and effective. The primary criteria should focus on the educational and therapeutic potential of the tool, ensuring it supports specific learning outcomes or therapeutic objectives. Safety is another non-negotiable aspect, which involves evaluating the security features of the digital tool to protect children's data and privacy. Finally, the tool's suitability for use in therapeutic settings must be assessed—this includes checking for user-friendly interfaces that children can navigate easily and ensuring that the content is age-appropriate and culturally sensitive.

Reviewing commonly used digital tools in play therapy involves a detailed examination of their applications and their efficacy, which can be substantiated through case studies and expert reviews. For instance, consider a digital storytelling app famous in therapeutic settings for its interactive and engaging content. While the app may excel in capturing children's attention and improving their narrative skills, critically assessing potential downsides is essential. Does the app allow for customization according to a child's specific needs? How does it handle personal data? Reviews and case studies can provide real-life insights into the tool's performance in various therapeutic scenarios, highlighting its strengths and limitations. This thorough evaluation helps therapists make informed decisions about incorporating such tools into their practice, ensuring that they complement traditional therapy methods effectively.

The risk of digital overstimulation is a growing concern, particularly with the increasing sophistication of multimedia content. Overstimulation can occur when children are exposed to excessive audiovisual elements, leading to sensory overload, reduced attention spans, and even disrupted sleep patterns. To mitigate these risks; it's essential to choose digital tools that offer adjustable settings for audio and visual outputs, allowing customization to a level that's comfortable and non-disruptive for each child. Tools that promote active rather than passive engagement— requiring thoughtful interaction instead of mere observation—are preferable. These tools ensure children remain engaged and cognitively stimulated without overwhelming their sensory systems.

Regular updates and adaptations of digital tools are essential to keep pace with technological advancements and evolving therapeutic needs. What works today may be less effective tomorrow, as new developments can introduce improved functionalities or new types of digital interactions. Staying informed about these changes and being willing to adapt chosen tools accordingly is crucial for maintaining the relevance and effectiveness of digital aids in therapy. This might mean updating software, incorporating new digital activities, or even phasing out tools that no longer meet the high standards of therapeutic efficacy and safety. By maintaining a dynamic approach to digital tool usage; therapists can ensure that their methods remain at the cutting edge of technology, providing the best possible support to their young clients.

As we turn the page from evaluating digital tools to broader considerations in play therapy, remember that technology is a tool, not a replacement for the human elements of therapeutic interaction. The careful selection, critical review, cautious use, and continual adaptation of digital tools will ensure they serve as valuable allies in the therapeutic journey, enhancing our ability to connect with and support children in their developmental paths. This thoughtful technology integration represents a response to a digital age and a commitment to improving therapeutic practice through every available means.

Conclusion

In this chapter, we've navigated the complex terrain of integrating digital tools into play therapy, emphasizing the importance of a balanced, thoughtful approach. From establishing criteria for tool selection to understanding the risks of digital overstimulation, the focus has been ensuring that digital interactions enrich the therapeutic environment without overshadowing the essential human elements. As we move forward into the next chapter, we carry with us the insights and strategies that will help us continue to harness the potential of digital tools responsibly and effectively, ensuring they complement rather than complicate the therapeutic goals we strive to achieve.

Chapter 5

Advanced Play Therapy Techniques

As you navigate the deeper waters of play therapy, this chapter introduces you to advanced techniques that further enhance your ability to foster meaningful connections and promote healing in children. Each child you encounter brings unique experiences and needs, so your approach must be equally nuanced and dynamic. Among these specialized techniques, Theraplay stands out as a profoundly impactful method, particularly in strengthening attachments and nurturing self-esteem in children who struggle with these aspects of their development.

5.1 Theraplay Techniques: Enhancing Attachment and Self-Esteem

Foundations of Theraplay

Theraplay is a guided play therapy that enhances the child's and caregiver's attachment. Developed in the 1960s by psychologist Ann Jernberg, Theraplay was inspired by the natural, healthy interaction patterns observed between parents and young children. These interactions, characterized by nurturing, challenge, engagement, and structure, are crucial in developing a secure attachment and a positive sense of self. Theraplay sessions are active, intense, and interpersonal, involving activities replicating these nurturing interactions under the therapist's guidance. This approach is particularly beneficial in addressing issues stemming from troubled attachment relationships, whether due to adoption, hospitalizations, or disruptions in the caregiver-child relationship.

Engagement Activities

Theraplay's activities mirror the natural, healthy interactions between a caring adult and a child. These include structured games, developmental challenges, and nurturing activities that are playful yet geared toward specific therapeutic goals. For instance, mirroring games are a staple of Theraplay, where the therapist and child may engage in a simple game of copycat, mimicking each other's movements and expressions. This enhances the child's attunement to social cues and promotes a sense of connection and understanding between the child and the therapist or caregiver.

Nurturing activities involve feeding, gentle rocking, or caring for a 'wounded' toy, encouraging the child to accept care and develop trust. Challenges are also integral, as they help build the child's competence and self-esteem, which are essential to creating a secure attachment. These include cooperative games where the child must rely on the therapist to achieve a goal, building trust, and teamwork. Each activity is designed to be short, success-oriented, and reciprocal, ensuring that the child remains engaged and experiences a sense of achievement and closeness.

Impact on Self-Esteem

The direct, physically engaging, and emotionally expressive nature of therapy significantly impacts a child's self-esteem. Through consistent positive interactions, where the child is treated with warmth, dignity, and playful engagement, they begin to internalize these positive experiences. The activities in therapy are designed to provide immediate feedback and success, reinforcing the child's sense of self-worth and capability. For a child who may feel inadequate or insecure, succeeding in a cooperative task or receiving nurturing care in a playful context can be incredibly affirming. Over time, these positive interactions build a foundation from which the child can positively view themselves and their relationships with others.

Case Studies

Consider the case of a young boy, Alex, who was adopted at the age of 6 and had difficulties in forming secure attachments with his new family. Traditional therapy had limited success, but through regular therapy sessions, Alex began to show remarkable progress. Activities like feeding a stuffed animal with his therapist and engaging in joint storytelling, where he would lead the narrative, helped Alex feel more secure and valued. His caregivers were also involved in the sessions, learning to engage with Alex in ways that supported his emotional needs. Over several months, Alex's behavior towards his caregivers changed from standoffish and distrustful to warm and cooperative, a testament to the power of structured, playful engagement in healing attachment wounds.

Theraplay's unique approach to enhancing attachment and self-esteem through playful, engaging activities offers a powerful tool in the play therapist's repertoire. As you continue to explore and apply these techniques, remember the profound impact that structured, nurturing play can have on a child's development and recovery. Each session is an opportunity to rebuild and strengthen the foundational relationships that support a healthy, happy upbringing. Through therapy, you address specific developmental challenges and foster an environment of joy, security, and growth for the children in your care.

5.2 Directive vs. Non-directive Play Therapy: Choosing the Right Approach

In the nuanced world of play therapy, understanding the distinction between directive and non-directive approaches is crucial for tailoring your interventions to meet the unique needs of each child. As the name suggests, directive play therapy involves more structured guidance from the therapist. This approach often uses specific therapeutic games or activities to elicit particular responses or address defined issues. The therapist actively directs the play, usually setting goals and leading the child toward them. This method can be particularly effective when working with children needing more guidance to engage in the therapeutic process or targeting specific behavioral or emotional objectives.

In contrast, non-directive play therapy allows the child greater autonomy to lead the session, with the therapist acting more as a facilitator than a director. This approach is grounded in the belief that children, given the right conditions, can work toward their own solutions. The therapist provides a variety of toys and materials that the child can use as they choose without specific directions or goals. This method can be incredibly effective for encouraging creativity and independence and helping children express themselves in a safe, controlled environment. It's particularly suited to uncovering deeper emotional issues that the child may not be consciously aware of or reluctant to discuss directly.

Several factors should guide your decision when deciding which approach to use. Consider the child's age, maturity, and temperament. Younger or less verbally communicative children benefit more from directive play, where structured activities can provide clarity and direction. Conversely, older children or those more introspective may find more significant benefits in non-directive play, which allows them more freedom to explore and express complex emotions. Additionally, consider the specific goals of therapy. Are you aiming to modify certain behaviors, or are you providing a space for the child to explore and understand their emotions? Your objectives help determine the level of structure and direction needed in the sessions.

Integrating both directive and non-directive approaches within your practice can offer a flexible framework that adapts to each child's dynamic needs. For example, you might start with a directive approach to establish routines and boundaries, then gradually shift to a more non-directive approach as the child becomes more comfortable in the therapeutic setting. This blend can be particularly effective, providing structure while honoring the child's natural capacity for self-directed healing.

Let's consider some examples to illustrate how these approaches work in practice. In a directive session, a therapist might use a board game to teach social skills. The game provides clear rules and objectives, guiding the conversation and interactions toward specific learning outcomes, such as taking turns or expressing feelings. In a non-directive session, the therapist might provide a sandbox and a variety of figures and let the child create their world. The therapist observes and perhaps asks open-ended questions based on the child's play, but the child largely determines the direction of the session. The outcomes here are less predictable but can lead to profound insights into the child's thoughts and emotions.

Both approaches have their merits and can lead to significant therapeutic outcomes when applied appropriately. By understanding and adeptly applying both directive and non-directive play therapy, you enhance your ability to meet the diverse needs of the children you work with, facilitating their path toward emotional resilience and psychological well-being. Through this thoughtful application of play therapy techniques, you not only adapt to the requirements of each case but also ensure that your interventions are as effective and supportive as possible, fostering an environment where children feel guided and empowered to overcome their challenges.

5.3 Sandtray Therapy: Exploring Inner Worlds Through Play

Sandtray therapy, a distinctive and dynamic form of play therapy, invites children to physically manifest their internal thoughts and emotions using a sandbox and a variety of miniature figures. This therapeutic technique allows children to construct their microcosm, representing their perceptions of the world and personal experiences. As they arrange and rearrange the sand and figures, they are not merely playing; they communicate in a profound, often non-verbal way, making the invisible visible and the unspeakable accessible.

The therapeutic benefits of sandtray therapy are extensive, particularly in its unique ability to access unconscious processes and facilitate the expression of difficult emotions. For many children, especially those who may not have the vocabulary or emotional insight to articulate their feelings and experiences, sand tray therapy offers a safe, creative outlet for their expression. Children manipulating the figures and the sand can often bypass their conventional defenses and reservations, revealing more profound thoughts and feelings through their symbolic play. This process can be particularly effective in resolving internal conflicts as the child externalizes their struggles, views them from new perspectives, and experiments with different resolutions. The sand's tactile nature and the figures' tangible quality help ground the experience, making abstract concepts more concrete and manageable. Setting up an environment conducive to free expression and deep exploration is essential for practical sandtray therapy sessions. The sandbox should be large enough to accommodate a wide range of scenarios but small enough to be manageable and not overwhelming. It should be filled with clean, fine sand that is pleasant to touch and easy to mold. The selection of miniature figures is equally essential; a diverse array of options should be available to ensure the child can find representations that resonate with their inner experiences. These might include figures of people, animals, fantasy creatures, trees, vehicles, and buildings. Each element should be chosen carefully to provide the child with ample opportunities for expression without directing or limiting their choices.

Interpreting a child's sand tray creation requires sensitivity and expertise. It is vital to approach this interpretation without assumptions or projections. Instead, therapists should gently encourage the child to narrate their creation, explaining the figures' significance and placements. This narrative process is crucial as it allows the child to make conscious of the unconscious thoughts and emotions that the sandtray has surfaced. The therapist's role is to listen attentively, ask open-ended questions, and reflect on the child's insights, helping them explore and understand their inner world more deeply.

The effectiveness of sandtray therapy can be illustrated through various case examples where children overcame emotional hurdles and reached deeper self-understanding. In one case, a young girl dealing with her parent's divorce used the sandtray to create two distinct worlds: chaotic and stormy, calm and sunny. Through her explanation, it became clear that she felt torn between the two separate lives she now led with each parent. The therapy sessions focused on helping her find ways to bridge these worlds in her sandtray, paralleling her emotional work to integrate and accept the changes in her family life. Another case involved a boy who repeatedly positioned a figure of a small child behind a fence. Over time, and through the narrative process, he revealed feelings of isolation and fear related to a bullying experience at school. The therapist worked with him to introduce protective figures and eventually to remove the fence, symbolizing a growing sense of safety and confidence.

Sandtray therapy, with its blend of creative expression, tactile engagement, and symbolic exploration, offers a powerful tool for children to express and work through complex emotions and experiences. Integrating this technique into your therapeutic practice provides children a profound way to explore their inner worlds, resolve conflicts, and express feelings that might otherwise remain hidden. This exploration fosters healing and empowers children, giving them a sense of mastery over their own narratives and emotional landscapes.

5.4 Dramatic Play and Role Play: Tools for Exploration and Expression

Dramatic play and role play serve as vital components in the developmental toolkit for children, offering a sandbox of psychological and emotional growth. These forms of 'play' are not just about entertainment but foundational activities that help children understand and navigate the world around them. During dramatic play, children take on roles beyond their everyday experiences, from pretending to be astronauts exploring outer space to doctors treating patients. This type of play allows children to step into different social roles, experiment with decision-making, and explore outcomes in a controlled, safe environment. In these imaginative scenarios, children learn not just about the world but also about themselves and their capacities for empathy, problem-solving, and emotional regulation.

Implementing role play in therapeutic sessions requires thoughtful setup and facilitation. As a therapist, you guide the child through various scenarios designed to elicit certain responses or teach specific skills. Setting up a scenario might involve creating a simple setup in the playroom, such as a mock grocery store or a doctor's office, and equipping it with relevant props. The key is to make these settings as accurate as possible to immerse the child in the role entirely. Guiding the child's interactions during the play involves a delicate balance of allowing them to explore while steering the narrative in ways that meet therapeutic goals. For example, if the goal is to improve the child's ability to wait their turn, you might create a role-play scenario where the child needs to wait in line at a store, providing gentle reminders and encouragement as they practice this skill.

Once the play session concludes, debriefing becomes an essential step. This involves discussing the play session with the child and exploring their thoughts and feelings during the activity. This reflection allows the child to connect the dots between their play experiences and real-life emotions and scenarios. For instance, if the child played a caregiver in the role play, discussing how they felt taking care of someone else can open up conversations about empathy, caring, and responsibility. This process reinforces the lessons learned during play and deepens the child's understanding and integration of these experiences.

Role and dramatic play are particularly effective in teaching emotional regulation and social skills. These forms of the game naturally create scenarios that provoke emotions such as frustration, excitement, or disappointment. Children can explore how to handle these emotions within the safe confines of play. For example, if a child becomes frustrated when a play scenario does not go as planned, this moment becomes a teachable opportunity. You can guide the child through strategies such as taking deep breaths, discussing alternative outcomes, or finding ways to solve the problem. Through these interactions, children learn that emotions are manageable and that they possess the tools to regulate them effectively.

Moreover, integrating dramatic play with other therapeutic modalities can significantly enhance treatment outcomes, especially in group therapy settings. In a group setting, dramatic play can be used to foster social interaction and teamwork. Each child could take on a different role within a play scenario, encouraging them to work together to achieve a common goal, whether putting on a play or building a structure. This interaction improves social skills and helps children learn to navigate interpersonal relationships and conflicts. For children dealing with social anxiety or difficulties in social interaction, such structured yet playful interactions can boost confidence and improve their ability to engage with peers.

Through these dynamic and interactive forms of play, you can guide children through complex emotional landscapes and social dynamics, enhancing their ability to navigate life's challenges with greater resilience and understanding. As you continue to employ these techniques, remember that each session is an opportunity to transform play into profound learning and growth, helping children not only to imagine but to build the skills they need for their diverse roles throughout their lives.

5.5 Integrating Mindfulness into Play: Practices for Awareness and Calm

The modern world, with its fast-paced and sometimes overwhelming demands, affects adults and children. Introducing mindfulness into the therapeutic setting, particularly within play therapy, offers a soothing balm to the often overstimulated young minds. At its core, mindfulness involves being present in the moment, aware of our thoughts, feelings, and sensations without judgment. This practice can be a vital tool for children, helping them manage stress, navigate their emotional landscapes, and enhance their focus in a world of distractions.

Mindful play activities are specifically designed to weave the principles of mindfulness into the natural engagement of play. This fusion creates a powerful therapeutic approach that fosters calm, focus, and self-regulation. Consider, for instance, the practice of mindful coloring. This activity, which involves coloring within intricate patterns or designs, encourages children to focus on the task at hand, noticing the choice of colors and the sensations of the coloring tools against paper. This focus helps to clear the mind of cluttering thoughts, anchoring the child in the present moment. Similarly, sensory walks, another mindful play activity, involve taking walks in nature or another calming environment where children are guided to notice and verbalize the sensory experiences around them—such as the feel of the ground under their feet, the sounds of birds, or the smell of grass. This heightens their sensory awareness and promotes a deep connection with the present moment, a cornerstone of mindfulness.

Guided imaginative play is another transformative activity where elements of mindfulness are embedded within the play narrative. In this activity, children might be guided through a story where they imagine visiting a calm, beautiful place, like a beach or a forest. They are encouraged to visualize the details of this place and notice the feelings that arise as they imagine themselves in this peaceful setting. This form of play taps into the child's natural capacity for imagination while teaching them how to use visualization for self-soothing and emotion regulation. The vivid, sensory-rich details help fully engage the child's attention, fostering a meditative, mindful state that can counter anxiety or agitation.

The benefits of integrating mindfulness into play therapy are substantial. Children who engage in mindful play activities often show improvements in attention, becoming better able to concentrate on tasks both in and out of the therapeutic setting. This improved focus can lead to better academic performance and more skillful engagement in social interactions, where sustained attention to social cues is crucial. Emotional regulation is another significant benefit. Mindful play teaches children how to observe their emotions without immediate reaction, allowing them to choose how they respond to their feelings. This skill mainly benefits children who experience intense emotions and may react impulsively. By managing their emotional responses, they gain greater control over their actions, leading to smoother interactions with peers and adults and better overall adjustment.

Teaching mindfulness to children through play requires a thoughtful approach, ensuring that activities are age-appropriate and engaging. The key is introducing mindfulness in a playful, light-hearted way that captures the child's interest. For younger children, this might involve short, simple activities with immediate, tangible outcomes, such as blowing bubbles to practice deep breathing. For older children, activities can involve more complex mindfulness practices, such as yoga poses combined with storytelling or creating personal mandalas that reflect their current emotional state. Integrating these practices into play therapy should be gradual and responsive to the child's curiosity and capacity, allowing them to explore these new skills at their own pace.

As you incorporate mindfulness into your play therapy sessions, you open up a new avenue for therapeutic engagement. This avenue offers children the tools to calm their minds, center their emotions, and fully engage with the present moment. These skills learned within the joy and creativity of play, equip children to handle the challenges of their worlds more effectively, promoting immediate well-being and long-term resilience.

5.6 Expressive Arts in Play Therapy: Using Creativity as a Therapeutic Tool

Expressive arts therapy integrates the use of art, music, dance, and drama into therapeutic practices, presenting a dynamic avenue for children to explore and express their emotions, often beyond what they can articulate in words. In the context of play therapy, expressive arts offer a multifaceted approach to addressing emotional and psychological challenges, making it an invaluable tool in your therapeutic repertoire. Through these artistic modalities, children can engage in activities that do more than entertain; they heal, communicate complex feelings, and foster significant personal development.

The therapeutic impact of artistic expression on children cannot be overstated. Art, whether painting, sculpting, or drawing, is a non-verbal language through which children can externalize deep-seated emotions, thoughts, and experiences. This form of expression can be remarkably liberating for children who may struggle with verbal communication or those who have experienced trauma. Music therapy allows children to explore rhythms and melodies that can soothe or stimulate, facilitating emotional regulation and expression. Dance therapy engages the body, allowing children to express feelings through movement, which can be especially powerful for kinesthetically inclined people. Drama and role-playing enable children to enact various roles and scenarios, providing them a safe space to explore different outcomes and emotional responses.

Implementing these artistic modalities in play therapy requires an environment that encourages creativity and expression without judgment. Providing various materials and opportunities for children to explore these different forms of expression is essential. For instance, an art station equipped with paints, clay, crayons, and construction paper invites visual and tactile exploration. A music corner with simple instruments like drums, xylophones, and maracas can engage children in auditory and rhythmic exploration. Incorporating elements like a small stage area or puppet theater can facilitate dramatic play. The key is to tailor these activities to the child's interests and therapeutic needs, ensuring that each child feels comfortable and motivated to express themselves creatively.

Case studies highlight the profound impact expressive arts can have in play therapy. For example, consider a case where a young girl, previously non-communicative following a traumatic event, began to use drawing as a means of expression during therapy sessions. Initially, her drawings were chaotic and dark, reflecting her inner turmoil. Over time, with gentle encouragement and validation of her art, she introduced brighter colors and structured forms, mirroring her emotional recovery. Another case involved a boy with autism who found social interactions challenging. Through music therapy, he connected with others by participating in group drumming sessions, which improved his ability to cooperate and communicate with peers.

As you integrate expressive arts into your play therapy sessions, remember that these activities are not just tools for expression but also therapeutic intervention opportunities. Each drawing, song, dance, or dramatic scene is a window into the child's inner world, offering insights that might not be accessible through conventional therapy techniques. By fostering an environment where children feel safe to express themselves creatively, you help them explore and resolve personal and emotional challenges and support their overall development and well-being.

As this chapter closes, reflect on the power of expressive arts in enriching play therapy. These creative modalities offer unique pathways to healing and growth, helping children articulate their deepest emotions and forge a path toward recovery and self-discovery. As you move forward, carry these insights into your continued exploration of play therapy techniques, ready to unlock new dimensions of therapeutic engagement that support and celebrate the resilience and creativity of the children you serve. Now, let us turn our attention to the next chapter, where we will explore the integration of family dynamics in play therapy, broadening our scope to include the pivotal role families play in the therapeutic journey of children.

Chapter 6

Play Therapy for Emotional and Social Development

Imagine a world where every child master the art of empathy, understands their emotions and navigates social interactions gracefully and confidently. In this chapter, we delve into how play therapy can be a pivotal tool in cultivating emotional intelligence—a critical aspect of a child's development that significantly influences their interpersonal skills and inner resilience. As you explore this chapter, consider how these playful, therapeutic approaches can be integrated into your interactions with children, whether you're a parent, educator, or therapist, to foster a deeper understanding and practice of emotional and social skills.

6.1 Emotional Intelligence Through Play: Activities That Teach Empathy and Awareness

Empathy Role-Playing

Empathy, the ability to understand and share the feelings of another, is a fundamental social skill. In play therapy, role-playing is a powerful method to enhance this skill. By engaging in role-playing games, children step into the shoes of others, experiencing scenarios from diverse perspectives. For instance, a child might take on the role of a sibling feeling left out or a friend who has lost a pet. These role-plays do more than teach children to recognize emotional cues; they immerse them in situations that require a thoughtful, empathetic response. As you guide a child through these role-playing sessions, gently prompt them to consider how the characters feel and why, reinforcing the connections between actions and emotional responses. This guided empathy deepens the child's emotional understanding and enhances their ability to navigate real-world relationships.

Emotion Matching Games

Emotion-matching games serve as an excellent tool to further build on emotional literacy. These games match facial expressions with corresponding emotions, helping children recognize and label feelings accurately. Use cards with different facial expressions or interactive digital apps for emotional education. As children pair happy faces with joy, sad faces with sorrow, or angry faces with frustration, they learn to identify subtle cues that signify various emotions. This recognition is crucial, as it forms the basis for empathetic interactions and emotional self-awareness. Regularly incorporating these games into play sessions helps children develop a vocabulary of emotions that can articulate their own feelings more clearly and understand those of others.

Interactive Storytelling

Interactive storytelling is another enriching activity that fosters emotional insight and creativity. In these sessions, children are invited to tell a story or modify an existing one, mainly focusing on the characters' emotions and potential outcomes. For example, if a story involves a character experiencing a setback, ask the child how that character might feel and explore different ways the character could respond. Encourage the child to alter the story's outcome, turning a negative situation into a positive one, stimulating emotional and creative thinking, and teaching resilience and problem-solving. These storytelling exercises are invaluable as they allow children to experiment with and understand the complexities of emotions in a narrative form, providing a safe space to explore different emotional scenarios and their consequences.

Feedback and Reflection

Integrating moments of feedback and reflection into play activities is essential for consolidating emotional learning. After a role-playing session or a storytelling exercise, take a moment to discuss with the child what emotions were explored and how various actions affected the characters in the scenario. Ask open-ended questions like, "How do you think the character felt when this happened?" or "What might you do if you were in a similar situation?" This dialogue encourages children to reflect on their emotional responses and understand the impact of their behaviors on others. These reflections are critical in helping children apply their emotional learning to their lives, enhancing their ability to empathize with others and navigate their social world with greater awareness and sensitivity.

Interactive Element: Emotion Journaling Prompt

To deepen the emotional learning process, introduce an emotion journaling prompt. After a play therapy session, encourage the child to draw or write about the feelings they explored during play. They might draw a scene from a role-play or write about how a particular story made them feel. This journaling acts as a reflective practice, allowing children to process and record their emotional experiences, which can be revisited and discussed in future sessions. This ongoing reflective practice reinforces the emotional concepts learned during play and promotes mindfulness and self-exploration that can support emotional well-being throughout life.

By weaving these activities into the fabric of play therapy, you provide children with a dynamic and supportive environment to learn about and practice emotional skills. These activities are not just games but are vital tools that equip children with the empathy, awareness, and emotional insight necessary for personal and interpersonal growth. As you continue to guide children through these playful yet profound experiences, you contribute to nurturing a generation that is emotionally intelligent, empathetic, and prepared to face the complexities of human emotions with confidence and understanding.

6.2 Social Skills Games: Fun Ways to Teach Interaction and Cooperation

Navigating the complex world of social interactions can be daunting for children, but integrating play into the learning process can transform these challenges into enjoyable and meaningful experiences. Social skills games are not merely activities; they are crucial building blocks that help children develop the ability to interact effectively, understand social norms, and build relationships based on mutual respect and understanding. Play therapy can significantly enhance a child's social competence through team-building activities, turn-taking games, communication exercises, and the strategic use of positive reinforcement.

Team-building exercises are essential in teaching children the value of cooperation and joint problem-solving. Engaging children in group puzzles or cooperative board games requires them to work together towards a common goal, fostering a sense of community and shared achievement. Imagine a game where children are tasked with building a structure using blocks, but each child can only use one hand. This scenario encourages them to assist each other and strategize collectively and highlights the importance of each member's role in achieving the group's objectives. Such activities encourage children to communicate openly, assign roles based on individual strengths, and support one another, which are fundamental aspects of effective teamwork. These skills are transferable to many areas of life, from academic group projects to maintaining healthy interpersonal relationships as they grow.

Turn-taking games are another pillar in the foundation of social skills, teaching children the virtues of patience and fairness. Games that require players to wait their turn, such as circle games or card games, help children understand the importance of giving everyone an equal opportunity to participate. These games often have rules that enforce fair play, which children must follow to continue participating. Adhering to these rules teaches children that fairness and respect for others' turns are valued behaviors in social interactions. Moreover, these games can be adapted for children of various ages and abilities, ensuring inclusivity and providing each child with a sense of belonging and contribution.

Communication exercises are pivotal in enhancing verbal and non-verbal communication skills. Activities like charades or partner storytelling games require children to convey information without words or to narrate stories in turns. For instance, children use gestures and expressions in charades to depict a word or phrase, while others guess the answer. This game not only hones their ability to express thoughts through body language but also enhances their interpretative skills, which are crucial for understanding non-verbal cues in real-life interactions. Partner storytelling, where children build on each other's narrative additions, promotes active listening and expressive speaking skills, fostering collaborative and respectful communication.

Positive reinforcement during these games can significantly influence children's behavior and attitudes towards social interactions. Recognizing and rewarding behaviors like sharing, polite communication, and respectful listening encourage children to repeat these behaviors. For instance, a child who patiently waits their turn or helps another during a team activity might be praised or given a small reward. This reinforcement is a powerful motivator for children, affirming that positive social interactions are appreciated and rewarded. Additionally, it helps children associate these behaviors with positive outcomes, increasing the likelihood that they will integrate these behaviors into their daily interactions.

By weaving these games and techniques into play therapy, you provide children with a fun and engaging way to learn and practice essential social skills. These activities prepare them to navigate the social world more effectively, enrich their relationships, and enhance their overall social experiences. As you guide children through these playful learning opportunities, you build their confidence and competence in interacting with the world around them, fostering a foundation of strong social skills that will benefit them throughout their lives.

6.3 Handling Bullying Through Play: Building Resilience and Confidence

In the dynamic landscape of a child's social interactions, bullying presents a significant challenge that can impact their emotional well-being and development. Play therapy, with its unique ability to engage children in meaningful activities, offers a powerful avenue to address and mitigate the effects of bullying. By incorporating role-playing for conflict resolution, resilience-building activities, discussion through puppetry, and facilitating peer support groups, play therapy can transform potentially traumatic experiences into opportunities for growth, empowerment, and connection.

Role-playing is an exceptionally effective tool because it allows children to simulate situations where they might encounter bullying. Under 'play' therapy's safe and controlled conditions, children can practice standing up for themselves or others, thereby boosting their assertiveness and confidence. For instance, a child might role-play a scenario where they witness a peer being teased. Guided by a therapist, the child can explore different ways to respond, from seeking an adult's help to addressing the bully calmly and assertively. These role-playing sessions equip children with practical skills and self-assurance to handle similar real-life situations. They learn that they have the power to influence their environment positively, which is a potent antidote to the feelings of helplessness that often accompany being bullied.

Building resilience is another critical aspect of play therapy focused on helping children cope with adversity. Designing activities that involve overcoming challenges, such as obstacle courses or problem-solving games, teaches children that obstacles can be overcome with persistence and creativity. As children navigate these physical and mental challenges, they internalize the understanding that setbacks can be temporary and surmountable. This realization fosters a resilient mindset, crucial for children who experience bullying, as it empowers them to face difficulties with a proactive and persistent attitude. Moreover, the success achieved in these activities provides a significant boost to their self-esteem, which is often eroded in bullying situations.

Puppetry offers a unique medium to discuss bullying scenarios and appropriate responses. Using puppets, a therapist can stage interactions that reflect everyday bullying situations, allowing children to observe and process the dynamics in a detached manner, which can be less intimidating than direct discussions. After the puppet show, the therapist can engage the children in a dialogue about what they observed, exploring feelings, identifying inappropriate behaviors, and discussing better ways to handle such situations. This method is particularly effective because puppets can make the scenarios less personal and more accessible, allowing children to express thoughts and emotions that might be difficult to articulate in a more direct conversation.

Finally, peer support groups within the play therapy framework can be instrumental in helping children cope with the emotional fallout of bullying. These groups provide a space where children can share their experiences with peers who may have faced similar challenges. Through guided activities encouraging sharing and mutual support, children learn that they are not alone in their experiences, which can be incredibly reassuring. The therapist can help facilitate discussions that foster empathy, support, and collective problem-solving. These interactions provide immediate emotional support and build a community of peers who can stand up for one another, reinforcing the idea that they can create a safer and more supportive social environment.

By integrating these approaches into play therapy, you, as a caregiver or therapist, provide children with the tools and support they need to navigate the challenges of bullying. The skills they learn—assertiveness, resilience, empathy, and mutual support—are strategies to handle bullying and invaluable life skills that will serve them well beyond their immediate circumstances. Through the thoughtful application of play therapy techniques, you can help transform a child's experience from victimization to empowerment and growth, fostering recovery and profoundly strengthening their character and interpersonal relationships.

6.4 Play Scenarios for Conflict Resolution: Teaching Children to Resolve Disputes

Conflicts are inevitable in the dynamic, often unpredictable playground of life. For children still mastering the art of social navigation, these conflicts can be notably perplexing and emotionally charged. Play therapy, with its unique blend of creativity and structured interaction, offers a sanctuary where children can learn the art of conflict resolution in a controlled, supportive environment. This sub-chapter explores innovative ways to weave conflict resolution skills into play, ensuring children learn to handle disputes effectively and carry these vital skills into everyday interactions.

Mediation Role Play

Role-playing as mediators provides children with a unique opportunity to step into the shoes of a neutral third party, a position that teaches them the invaluable skills of negotiation and peacemaking. Set up scenarios that mirror common conflicts children might face, such as disputes over sharing toys or choosing group activities. In these role-plays, children are guided to act as mediators, helping their peers navigate the conflict toward a peaceful resolution. This method teaches children to listen actively, understand different perspectives, and facilitate a dialogue that encourages compromise and consensus. For example, in a mediation role-play, one child might suggest, "How about we take turns playing with the toy? Each can have it for five minutes." This practice enhances their ability to resolve disputes and boosts their confidence in handling similar situations in their social circles.

Problem-Solving Games

Games that require collective problem-solving can also be instrumental in teaching peaceful conflict resolution.

Introduce games where the goal can only be achieved through cooperative efforts, and each player's contribution is crucial to the group's success. These might include strategy games that require players to work together to solve a puzzle or construct a device that performs a specific function. During these activities, conflicts naturally arise, providing perfect teachable moments. Facilitators can guide the group through these conflicts by encouraging open communication, where each child expresses their ideas and frustrations in a respectful manner, and by steering the group toward collaborative solutions. Working together to solve a problem cements the concept of teamwork and subtly reinforces the notion that many conflicts can be resolved through cooperative effort and creative thinking.

Emotion Regulation Techniques in Play

Integrating emotion regulation techniques into play scenarios is crucial, as conflicts often evoke strong emotions. Teach children simple, effective strategies to manage their feelings during heated moments, such as deep breathing, counting to ten, or using positive self-talk. These techniques can be gamified to make them more engaging for children. For example, create a 'cool down' race where children practice slowing their breathing to lower the number of breaths they take per minute or a counting game where children count backward from twenty during a frustrating moment in a game. By practicing these techniques in a playful context, children learn to associate them with positive outcomes, making it more likely that they will utilize these strategies during real-life conflicts.

Reflection and Learning

Finally, dedicate time for reflection and discussion after each conflict resolution scenario. This practice allows children to process what happened, discuss the emotions they experienced, and evaluate the effectiveness of the resolution strategies used. Ask guided questions like, "How did it feel when you found a solution?" or "What could we try differently next time?" This helps solidify the lessons learned and encourages ongoing improvement and a deeper understanding of conflict dynamics. Facilitators can use this time to reinforce key concepts and praise positive behaviors, such as effective communication or emotional control, further motivating children to continue using these skills.

Through these carefully designed play scenarios, children learn that conflicts, while challenging, can be navigated successfully and respectfully. They gain the skills to resolve disputes and better understand themselves and others, fostering empathy and cooperation beyond the playroom. As you guide children through these play-based learning experiences, you contribute to their growth into empathetic, thoughtful individuals capable of handling life's conflicts with poise and understanding.

6.5 Celebrating Diversity: Games That Teach Inclusion and Respect

In a world as interconnected as ours, understanding and embracing diversity isn't just a virtue but a necessity. This understanding starts early in life, and as a stakeholder in children's development—whether as a parent, educator, or therapist—you hold the keys to unlocking a broader perspective in young minds. Introducing children to the vast tapestry of cultures, experiences, and perspectives through play enriches their understanding and plants the seeds of respect and empathy essential for navigating a diverse world. Let's explore how you can integrate diversity into play therapy, creating a vibrant learning environment that celebrates differences and fosters acceptance.

Cultural Exchange Activities

One of the most joyful ways to introduce children to different cultures is through play activities celebrating various global traditions. Imagine organizing an international food-tasting game where children can experience flavors from around the world, turning what could be a simple snack time into a lively exploration of tastes and traditions. Each food item can be paired with a story or a fun fact about the country it comes from, making the experience both educational and gastronomically delightful. Similarly, hosting a world music dance party can be an exhilarating way for children to feel the rhythms of different cultures, from the energetic drumbeats of West African music to the soothing melodies of Andean flutes. These activities do more than expose children to other cultures; they engage their senses, making the learning process deeply immersive and memorable. By weaving these experiences into play therapy sessions, you help children appreciate the richness of the world's cultures in a setting that is filled with fun and excitement.

Inclusive Role-Playing

Role-playing games are a staple in play therapy for their versatility and effectiveness in teaching various skills, from empathy to problem-solving. To infuse these games with lessons on diversity and inclusion, consider creating scenarios with characters from diverse backgrounds and situations requiring understanding and respecting differences. For instance, a role-playing game might involve characters who speak different languages trying to find ways to communicate and collaborate to solve a puzzle. Another scenario could be about characters from other parts of the world sharing their local customs and finding common ground. These role-playing sessions encourage children to think creatively and empathetically about differences, promoting a deeper understanding of diversity and teaching them how to interact respectfully with people who might look, speak, or live differently than they do.

Empathy-Building Stories and Plays

Stories and plays are potent tools for building empathy, allowing children to 'live' experiences different from their own. By using narratives that highlight diverse experiences and challenges, you can help children understand and feel connected to realities that differ from theirs. For example, a play could depict a day in a child's life from another country, including their challenges, such as dealing with natural disasters or navigating cultural festivals. Alternatively, a story session could focus on historical figures from diverse backgrounds who have significantly contributed to society. These stories not only expand children's knowledge about the world but also build a bridge of empathy, helping them to understand and respect the struggles and achievements of others.

Group Discussions

After engaging in play activities that explore diversity, facilitating group discussions can help reinforce the lessons learned. These discussions can be guided by thoughtful questions and prompts that encourage children to reflect on what they learned and how it applies to their interactions with others. For example, after a storytelling session about a character from a different cultural background, you might ask the children how they think the character feels about certain events in the story or what they would do if they met someone like the character. These discussions can be invaluable for consolidating understanding and appreciation for diversity, allowing children to express their thoughts and feelings about new concepts and cultures they've encountered through play.

By integrating these diverse and culturally rich activities into play therapy, you broaden children's horizons and lay a strong foundation for empathy, respect, and a deep-seated appreciation for the richness different cultures bring to our collective human experience. As children learn to celebrate diversity through play, they carry these values into their everyday lives, enriching their interactions and contributing to a more inclusive and respectful society.

6.6 Play Interventions for Anxiety and Depression: Gentle Approaches for Tough Emotions

For children grappling with the shadows of anxiety and depression, the therapeutic power of play offers a beacon of light. It's a realm where structured, soothing activities blend with the creative expression of deep-seated emotions, providing a sanctuary for healing. It's essential to tailor these activities to resonate with the sensitivities of such children, fostering an environment where they can find solace, expression, and eventual empowerment over their emotional state.

Relaxation and mindfulness activities stand out as pivotal in this therapeutic journey. Incorporating techniques like guided imagery or progressive muscle relaxation into play sessions can significantly attenuate the symptoms of anxiety and depression by fostering a sense of calm and control. Picture a session where children are guided through a visualization of a tranquil forest, with each detail—the scent of the trees, the softness of the moss, the gentle rustle of leaves—crafted to draw them deeper into a state of peace. Alternatively, progressive muscle relaxation can be introduced through a storytelling format where children tighten and relax muscles to help a character prepare for a restful sleep after an adventurous day. These techniques not only help in reducing immediate feelings of anxiety but also equip children with tools they can use outside the therapy session to manage stress.

Expression through art offers another profound avenue for children to explore and articulate feelings that might be too complex or frightening to verbalize. Art-based play activities like drawing, sculpting, or painting provide a non-verbal outlet for emotions, allowing children to externalize what they feel in a form that can be observed, acknowledged, and discussed. This process validates their feelings and helps them understand and categorize their emotions, which is a crucial step toward managing them effectively. For instance, using colors to represent different feelings can help children show the intensity and mixture of their emotions, leading to insights both for them and the therapist about triggers and the nature of their emotional experiences.

Establishing routine and predictability in play therapy sessions imparts a sense of security that is immensely comforting to children suffering from anxiety.

When children know what to expect in a therapy session, it alleviates their apprehension and helps them engage more fully in the activities. This could be as simple as starting each session with a welcome song, followed by a brief discussion of the day's activities, and ending with a calming ritual like a few minutes of deep breathing or a reflective conversation about what they enjoyed most. This predictability makes the therapy space a haven for these children and teaches them the value of structure in managing unpredictable emotions.

Supportive peer play is invaluable, particularly for children dealing with depression, who often feel isolated in their struggles. Creating opportunities for supportive interactions in play settings allows children to give and receive encouragement and understanding. Facilitating small group activities where children can share experiences, work together on a joint project, or enjoy a game can significantly lessen feelings of loneliness and misunderstanding. These peer interactions, guided by the therapist to ensure they remain positive and supportive, help build a community around the child. This community understands, supports, and uplifts each member through shared experiences and mutual empathy.

These gentle yet powerful interventions weave together to form a comprehensive approach to tackling anxiety and depression through play therapy. Play therapy helps illuminate a path forward for children navigating the challenging terrain of these emotional conditions by engaging the body and mind in activities that soothe, express, and connect. Each session adds a stone to the foundation of their resilience, helping them build the strength to face life with renewed hope and improved emotional health.

The thoughtful integration of these play therapy techniques not only addresses the symptoms of anxiety and depression but also fosters an environment of understanding, support, and development for children. As they learn to navigate their emotions and interact positively with peers, they gain critical skills for immediate relief and long-term emotional well-being. This chapter has explored various ways to enrich the therapeutic journey for children affected by these emotional challenges, ensuring they have access to the tools and support needed to lead happier, more balanced lives. The principles and practices laid out here will continue to guide and inform effective therapeutic interventions, contributing to a broader understanding of the transformative power of play in healing and development.

Chapter 7

Addressing Behavioral Challenges through Play

In the tapestry of childhood development, behavioral challenges such as aggression and withdrawal often stand out, sometimes overshadowing a child's myriad other qualities. These behaviors, while challenging, are usually children's ways of communicating more profound distress, discomfort, or dissatisfaction with their environment. Understanding and addressing these behaviors through play offers a compassionate avenue for resolution and transformation. This chapter delves into nuanced play interventions that aim to mitigate these behaviors and to understand and transform them, fostering a nurturing bridge to emotional and social competence.

7.1 Play Interventions for Aggression and Withdrawal

Identifying Triggers Through Play

Navigating the complexities of aggressive or withdrawn behaviors in children begins with understanding the triggers behind these actions. Play, in its dynamic form, serves as a revealing lens into the child's world, offering cues and clues that might be invisible in more conventional settings. You can map out distress patterns and triggers by observing a child's interactions with toys and their responses to various play scenarios. For instance, a child might exhibit aggression when losing a game or might withdraw when certain toys are introduced, indicating areas of sensitivity or past trauma. These observations are pivotal as they guide the therapeutic direction, helping you tailor interventions that address specific emotional triggers. The key lies in watchful observation, patience, and readiness to perceive play beyond mere activity, seeing it as a language through which the child communicates their deepest feelings and fears.

Role-Playing Conflict Resolution

Role-playing is a powerful tool in the play therapist's kit, especially for children struggling with aggression or withdrawal. Children can experiment with social roles and responses through role-play in a safe, controlled environment. This method allows them to step into another's shoes and understand other perspectives or practice assertive communication and conflict resolution skills without real-world consequences. For a child prone to aggression, role-playing as a character who navigates a conflict peacefully can provide new behavioral strategies and insights. For the withdrawn child, assuming a role that requires active engagement can boost confidence and social skills. The beauty of role-play lies in its flexibility—scenarios can be crafted to meet each child's unique developmental and therapeutic needs, making it an invaluable strategy in moderating challenging behaviors.

Therapeutic Games for Emotional Regulation

Therapeutic games designed to aid in emotional regulation are critical, particularly for children who express themselves through extremes like aggression or withdrawal. For instance, integrating simple breathing exercises into a game of tag can help a child learn to manage excitement and physiological arousal playfully. Storytelling games, where children create narratives about overcoming fear or anger, can also be instrumental. These games allow children to explore different emotional outcomes in a fictional context, which can be translated into real-life emotional skills. These games aim to make learning emotional regulation skills engaging and integrated, ensuring that children adopt these skills not as imposed rules but as natural responses to emotional states.

Success Stories of Transformation

To illustrate the impact of these play-based interventions, consider the case of Jonah, a nine-year-old boy who exhibited severe withdrawal and anxiety in social settings. Through targeted play interventions focusing on role-playing and storytelling, Jonah gradually began to express himself and engage with peers. His breakthrough came during a role-playing session where he portrayed a hero who had to negotiate peace between conflicting parties. This role allowed him to practice assertiveness and conflict resolution, making noticeable improvements in real-world interactions. Another case is that of Eliza, who displayed frequent bursts of aggression. Through play that identified triggers and taught emotional regulation, Eliza learned to recognize signs of frustration early and use calming techniques effectively. These stories underscore the transformative potential of play therapy, not just in altering behaviors but in empowering children with the skills to navigate their emotional landscapes more successfully.

Interactive Element: Reflective Journal Prompt

Consider incorporating a reflective journaling exercise for parents or caregivers. After a play therapy session, take a moment to write down any noticeable behaviors or triggers observed in the child. Reflect on how different play activities influenced the child's behavior and consider any changes or adaptations that might benefit future sessions. This practice enhances understanding of the child's behavioral patterns and actively involves caregivers in the therapeutic process, fostering a collaborative approach to overcoming behavioral challenges.

Through the thoughtful application of these play interventions, we move beyond merely managing symptoms to understanding and transforming the underlying causes of challenging behaviors. This chapter equips you with practical strategies and encourages a deeper engagement with the child's emotional world, paving the way for meaningful and lasting change.

7.2 Setting Boundaries within Play

In the dynamic landscape of play therapy, establishing consistent boundaries forms the bedrock of a secure and predictable environment, essential for a child's therapeutic progress. Boundaries in play therapy are not just about rules and limitations; they are about creating a structured space where children can explore their emotions and behaviors safely and confidently. These boundaries help children understand what is expected of them and what they can expect from others, which is crucial in building trust and a sense of security. When children know the limits and rules, they are more likely to engage deeply, as this structure reduces anxiety and confusion, making the therapeutic environment more predictable. For instance, clear boundaries regarding how and when to use certain toys can prevent conflicts and help children navigate their interactions more smoothly, fostering a sense of control and respect for the shared space and resources.

Games that teach boundary setting are instrumental in helping children understand and respect personal and social boundaries. One practical approach involves using physical spaces within games to delineate personal boundaries. For example, using hula hoops or chalk lines to create individual 'zones' during a group game helps children visually comprehend and respect personal space. This can be particularly beneficial in teaching children who struggle with spatial awareness or may not understand non-verbal cues indicating someone's discomfort with physical closeness. Similarly, rule-based games like 'Simon Says' or 'Red Light, Green Light' are excellent for teaching social boundaries. These games require listening and responding to specific instructions, helping children learn the importance of observing social rules and the consequences of not adhering to them. Through these playful yet structured activities, children learn the valuable skills of boundary recognition and respect, which are fundamental to social interaction and personal respect.

Engaging children in the rule-making process is another transformative strategy in play therapy. When children are involved in setting the rules for play, they are more likely to understand and respect these boundaries because they own them. This process empowers children, giving them a voice and a sense of agency that can be particularly healing for those who may feel powerless in other areas of their lives. For instance, before a play session, you might discuss with the child what rules should apply to using toys. The child's input on sharing and caring for the toys teaches responsibility and instills a sense of fairness and cooperation. Such involvement makes the rules more meaningful and respected and enhances the child's understanding of why boundaries are necessary, promoting a deeper internalization of these concepts.

Handling boundary violations during play offers significant teaching moments. Strategies for addressing these violations should focus on correction through understanding rather than punishment, ensuring the child learns from the experience without feeling discouraged from future participation. For example, if a child repeatedly grabs toys from others, instead of an immediate reprimand, you could use this moment to pause the game and discuss feelings. Asking questions like, "How do you think it makes your friend feel when you take their toy without asking?" helps the child understand the impact of their actions. You could then guide the child to apologize and ask for the toy properly, reinforcing the learning through positive feedback when they follow the revised approach. Such interventions address the immediate behavior and teach essential skills of empathy, respect, and conflict resolution, which are invaluable beyond the play therapy sessions.

These structured yet flexible approaches to setting and enforcing boundaries within play therapy maintain the session's therapeutic integrity and teach children essential life skills. Children learn to navigate their worlds more effectively through consistent boundaries, engaging games, participatory rule-making, and thoughtful handling of violations, making play therapy a profoundly transformative experience in their developmental journey.

7.3 Games that Teach Social Rules and Norms

In child development, mastering social rules and norms is not just about learning how to behave in society—it's about understanding how to interact respectfully, cooperatively, and compassionately. Play provides a natural, engaging platform for teaching these essential life skills. Children can learn everything through carefully designed play activities, from taking turns and cooperating to understanding more complex social cues and norms. This enhances their immediate social interactions and builds lifelong social competence and emotional intelligence.

One effective strategy for teaching social rules through play involves cooperative board games. These games require players to work together toward a common goal rather than competing against one another. For example, a game where players must collaborate to solve a puzzle or complete a task before a timer runs out encourages teamwork, communication, and joint problem-solving. Through these games, children learn the value of listening to others, contributing to a team effort, and experiencing the joy of shared success. Another enriching activity is role-playing, which allows children to enact various social scenarios in a controlled environment. Children can explore multiple social interactions and outcomes by taking on different roles. For instance, role-playing in a classroom where each child takes turns being the teacher or a student helps them understand and respect different roles and perspectives. The therapist can guide these role-play sessions to introduce conflicts or challenges that require cooperative solutions, teaching children how to negotiate and compromise effectively.

Incorporating feedback and reflection into play activities significantly enhances the learning process. After a cooperative game or role-play session, discussing what happened during the play teaches children to reflect on their behavior and social interactions. This can be structured as a simple group discussion where each child shares what they enjoyed about the activity, what challenges they faced, and how they felt about the interactions. For example, after a role-play session, you might ask children what they thought about waiting for their turn to speak or how they felt when others helped them in a game. This reflection deepens their understanding of social dynamics and encourages self-assessment and emotional insight. This feedback must be framed positively and constructively, focusing on what children can learn from each experience rather than what they did wrong.

Evaluating progress in social skills is an essential part of play therapy, ensuring that the interventions are effective and that children are developing in their ability to navigate social situations. Observing children in group play settings provides invaluable insights into their social skills development. For instance, you might note improvements in how a child negotiates roles in a play activity or handles losing a game. These observations can be supplemented with more structured assessments, such as having caregivers or teachers provide feedback on the child's social interactions outside therapy sessions. Additionally, engaging children in discussions about their perceptions of their social interactions can provide further insights into their self-awareness and the impact of the play therapy. By regularly assessing these areas, you can tailor future play activities to address specific social learning needs, ensuring that each child continues to develop robust social skills that will serve them throughout their lives.

Through these play-based strategies, children are not just learning social rules; they are experiencing and practicing them in real time, which embeds these skills more deeply than passive learning ever could. The beauty of using play this way is that it feels less like instruction and more like exploration, making learning a joyous, naturally social experience.

7.4 Reward Systems in Play: Do's and Don'ts

Incorporating reward systems into play therapy can motivate children, steering them towards positive behaviors and reinforcing their engagement in therapeutic activities. However, the key to a successful reward system is its thoughtful assembly and balanced execution. Understanding the difference between intrinsic and extrinsic motivation is crucial. Intrinsic motivation arises within the child, driven by an internal desire to engage in a task for its own sake, leading to autonomous behaviors. On the other hand, extrinsic motivation involves external rewards such as stickers, praise, or tokens, which can be highly effective but should not become the sole reason a child engages in therapy.

It's essential to balance these two forms of motivation to use rewards in play therapy effectively. This balance ensures that while children appreciate and strive for external rewards, they also find joy and satisfaction in the activities, fostering a more profound, intrinsic connection to their therapeutic journey. For instance, integrating rewards that directly relate to the play activity, such as earning a puzzle piece for every cooperative interaction during a group activity, can help link the reward to the intrinsic enjoyment and accomplishment of the play. This reinforces the desired behavior and enhances the child's engagement with the activity, making the therapy more effective.

Designing a reward system that is fair, transparent, and aligned with therapeutic goals requires meticulous planning. Token systems can be particularly effective when children earn tokens for specific behaviors and exchange them for privileges or small rewards. These systems provide clear and consistent feedback to children about their behavior, making the abstract concept of 'progress' tangible. For instance, earning a token for each day the child practices a new coping skill provides immediate positive reinforcement and a visual representation of their achievements. It's imperative, however, that such systems are transparent—children should understand how and why they earn tokens and what they can expect when they redeem them. This transparency helps build trust and ensures the child sees the reward system as fair and directly related to their efforts.

However, there are pitfalls to avoid when implementing reward systems in play therapy. An over-reliance on material rewards can lead to a situation where the child's motivation is tied solely to what they receive rather than the satisfaction and growth derived from the therapeutic activities. This external focus can diminish the intrinsic value of therapy, making it harder for the child to engage in the absence of rewards. Moreover, creating a competitive environment, especially in group settings, can inadvertently foster feelings of inadequacy or aggression among children, counteracting the collaborative and supportive nature of therapy. It is crucial, therefore, to monitor the impact of any reward system and ensure it fosters a supportive atmosphere, emphasizing personal growth and cooperation over competition.

Tailoring reward systems to meet the diverse motivational needs of children ensures that the rewards are meaningful and effective. This customization involves observing each child's responses and preferences and possibly adjusting the rewards to suit their motivational drivers better. For a child who values social recognition, verbal praise or leadership in a group activity might be more motivating than tangible rewards. Another child might find a selection of privileges, like choosing a game or leading a session activity, more compelling. This individualized approach enhances the reward system's effectiveness and shows each child that their unique preferences and needs are acknowledged and valued.

In implementing these strategies, it's vital to remember that the ultimate goal of any reward system should be to foster a positive therapeutic environment, encouraging growth, learning, and genuine engagement. By carefully constructing and managing reward systems, you can enhance the therapeutic experience, making it more enjoyable and impactful for the children involved.

As we wrap up this exploration of reward systems in play therapy, remember that the valid reward lies in the children's progress. The techniques and strategies discussed here are tools to guide and enhance this developmental journey, each tailored to fit the unique narrative of every child's therapeutic needs. Moving forward, the insights garnered here will serve as a foundation for more nuanced interactions and interventions, ensuring that play therapy remains a dynamic and enriching experience for all involved.

Chapter 8

Case Studies and Real-World Applications

In the dynamic field of play therapy, where abstract theories meet the tangible world, the true impact of our work unfolds in the transformational stories of the children we serve. This chapter is dedicated to bringing these stories into the light—not just as testimonies of change but as beacons for all embarking on this therapeutic path. Here, you'll find the essence of play therapy brought to life through detailed narratives, showcasing the profound influence of thoughtful, creative therapeutic interventions on children's lives. These stories are not merely accounts of overcoming challenges but narratives of empowerment, resilience, and, most importantly, hope.

8.1 From Theory to Practice: Real-World Success Stories of Play Therapy

Documentation of Transformational Stories

In the heart of a bustling city, a seven-year-old boy named Lucas found his sanctuary within the colorful walls of a community center. Struggling with severe anxiety and social withdrawal after his parent's divorce, Lucas initially communicated only through whispers and would not make eye contact. His play therapist introduced him to a puppet theater, where Lucas could project his feelings onto inanimate characters, expressing his fears and hopes through puppetry. Over months of sessions, Lucas gradually began to express himself more openly, using the puppets to narrate stories that mirrored his internal struggles. By externalizing his emotions in a controlled, playful environment, he learned to confront and manage his feelings. The outcome was profound: Lucas returned to being an active participant in his classroom and began initiating playdates with peers, a significant breakthrough in his social interaction and emotional expression.

Therapist Narratives

Sophia, a seasoned play therapist, shares her experience with an eight-year-old girl, Mia, who was referred to therapy for aggression and defiance. Through the lens of non-directive play therapy, Sophia provided Mia with a space filled with diverse play options yet observed that Mia was consistently drawn to a set of building blocks. Mia would build elaborate structures only to destroy them in apparent frustration. Recognizing this repetitive pattern, Sophia gently introduced narrative play, encouraging Mia to create stories about her constructions. As Mia narrated tales of homes being destroyed by storms and subsequently rebuilt, Sophia guided her to draw parallels with her feelings about her family's recent relocation. This breakthrough led Mia to process her anger and confusion, ultimately helping her cope with the significant changes in her life.

Variety of Settings

Play therapy thrives in various settings, each offering unique advantages that cater to children's needs. In clinical settings, therapists like John utilize one-way mirrors for parental observation, providing immediate feedback and fostering a collaborative approach to addressing behavioral issues. In schools, therapists integrate play therapy into the classroom, helping children like Emma, who struggles with attention deficit hyperactivity disorder (ADHD), to engage in focused, goal-oriented activities that enhance her academic and social skills. Community centers, on the other hand, offer a more relaxed environment where group play therapy sessions help children like Leo, who has post-traumatic stress disorder (PTSD), find a sense of community and support among peers with similar experiences.

Impact Measurement

Evaluating the success of play therapy interventions is crucial for validating the approach and refining techniques to serve the children's needs better. Behavioral assessments, such as the Child Behavior Checklist (CBCL), provide quantifiable data on changes in behavior and emotional states. Collected through structured interviews or questionnaires, feedback from parents and teachers offers additional qualitative insights into the child's progress in real-world settings. For instance, after several months of play therapy, feedback on Lucas highlighted his newfound confidence and reduced anxiety, corroborating the observations made during sessions. This multi-source feedback system ensures a comprehensive view of the child's transformation, guiding ongoing adjustments to the therapeutic approach to maximize benefits.

Interactive Element: Reflective Journal Prompt

Consider a child you know who might be struggling emotionally or behaviorally. Reflect on how a tailored play therapy intervention could transform their coping mechanisms and well-being. What changes would you hope to see, and how could they be measured in therapy and their everyday environment?

Through these real-world examples and insights from practicing therapists, this chapter illuminates the tangible impacts of play therapy, underscoring its versatility and efficacy across various settings and conditions. Each story serves as a testament to the children's resilience and as inspiration for therapists, caregivers, and educators who play pivotal roles in these transformative journeys. As we explore further case studies and applications, let these narratives remind you of play therapy's profound potential in reshaping young lives. Through strategic interventions, empathetic engagement, and creative expression, play therapy continues to unlock new pathways for healing and growth, making every session a stepping stone towards a brighter, more hopeful future for each child engaged in this therapeutic journey.

8.2 Overcoming Behavioral Challenges: Case Studies in Play Therapy

In the nuanced arena of child behavior, where symptoms like aggression, withdrawal, or hyperactivity signal deeper struggles, play therapy offers a profound avenue for transformation. Consider the case of Sarah, a ten-year-old girl whose aggression at school alarmed her teachers and peers alike. Initially, her outbursts seemed inexplicable, sparking concerns about behavioral disorders. However, through the lens of play therapy, a different story unfolded—one rooted in frustration and miscommunication rather than inherent defiance.

Sarah's therapist employed various play therapy techniques, beginning with therapeutic storytelling. Sarah was encouraged to create stories from pictures of ambiguous family scenes in sessions. This activity allowed her to project her feelings and experiences, revealing narratives of conflict and misunderstanding that mirrored her real-life frustrations. These pivotal sessions provided insights into Sarah's perspective that she couldn't articulate in conventional conversations. As understanding grew, role-playing became an integral tool. Sarah and her therapist enacted various outcomes to the conflicts in her stories, exploring strategies for expressing anger appropriately and resolving disputes without aggression. This method helped Sarah develop these skills and boosted her confidence in handling interpersonal conflicts.

Collaboration with caregivers was crucial in Sarah's therapy. Regular meetings with Sarah's parents and teachers were held to discuss her progress and strategize on reinforcing the coping mechanisms she learned during treatment. These discussions often modified how adults responded to Sarah's signs of frustration, promoting a consistent and supportive approach across her environments. The adults learned to recognize when Sarah might feel overwhelmed and how to intervene constructively, preventing escalations into aggression.

The long-term outcomes of Sarah's play therapy were significant and heartening. Follow-up assessments over the next year showed a marked decrease in her aggressive responses at school, and feedback from her teachers noted improved interactions with her classmates. These changes were not just behavioral adjustments but were indicative of a deeper emotional and psychological growth, highlighting the enduring impact of play therapy when coupled with supportive home and school environments.

Turning to another scenario, we meet Danny, an eight-year-old boy whose hyperactivity and inability to focus hindered his academic performance and social interactions. His play therapy journey began with expressive arts, utilizing drawing and clay modeling as mediums for him to express his energy and burgeoning thoughts. While seemingly simple, these activities were strategically chosen to help Danny channel his restlessness into creative endeavors, providing him with a sense of accomplishment and calmness.

Interactive games that required Danny to follow the rules and wait his turn were gradually introduced, enhancing his ability to control impulses and pay attention during structured activities. These games' tactile and engaging nature served dual purposes—maintaining his interest and subtly boosting his self-regulation skills. His parents were involved every step of the way, participating in sessions designed to teach them how to continue these activities at home, ensuring that the therapy's benefits extended beyond the clinical setting.

The assessment of Danny's progress was multifaceted, incorporating feedback from his teachers regarding his classroom behavior and his parents' observations at home. Over several months, there was a noticeable improvement in Danny's ability to engage in prolonged activities and interact more calmly with his peers. These outcomes underscored the effectiveness of integrating sensory and rule-based play therapies tailored to meet specific behavioral challenges, demonstrating the adaptability and impact of play therapy techniques in fostering significant behavioral and emotional growth.

8.3 Innovations in Play Therapy: Cutting-Edge Techniques and Their Outcomes

In the evolving landscape of play therapy, integrating technology has sparked a new wave of innovative approaches, broadening the horizons for therapeutic intervention. Among these, virtual reality (VR) play therapy and digital game-based therapy stand out as revolutionary tools that have begun to reshape traditional methods, offering immersive and engaging experiences that captivate children's interest while providing substantial therapeutic benefits. VR play therapy, for instance, immerses children in environments meticulously crafted to simulate real-life scenarios or fantastical worlds. This controlled, immersive experience is captivating and versatile, allowing therapists to tailor scenarios specifically targeting a child's therapeutic needs. Digital game-based therapy, on the other hand, utilizes the interactive and rewarding nature of video games to motivate and engage children in therapeutic tasks, turning the challenging process of therapy into an enjoyable journey of self-discovery and skill development.

The rationale behind these innovations is grounded in the understanding that today's children are digital natives born into a world where technology plays a significant role in their daily lives. By integrating these familiar elements into therapy, we speak their language and enhance their engagement and investment in the therapeutic process. These methods leverage the captivating power of digital environments to maintain the child's interest and focus, which is especially beneficial in addressing issues like attention deficits or high anxiety, where traditional therapy might struggle to retain the child's engagement.

Consider the case of Emily, an eleven-year-old girl dealing with social anxiety, which made it incredibly difficult for her to interact with peers in a traditional therapy setting. Emily's therapist decided to introduce VR play therapy, creating a virtual classroom setting where Emily could interact with avatars. Initially, the therapist controlled these avatars, but gradually, peers from her actual classroom were invited to join the virtual space. This innovative approach allowed Emily to practice social interactions in a safe, controlled environment, reducing her anxiety and gradually building her confidence. The outcomes were remarkable; Emily's ability to engage with her peers increased significantly, and her social anxiety scores, as measured by standardized psychological assessments, showed substantial improvement.

This leads to a comparative analysis of traditional versus innovative techniques in similar cases. While immensely beneficial, traditional play therapy can sometimes be limited by the physical confines of the therapy room or the resources available. In contrast, innovative techniques such as VR expand these boundaries, offering a limitless array of environments and scenarios. For children like Emily, who might find real-world interactions overwhelming, VR provides a gradual, controlled exposure that is not easily replicated in a traditional setting. However, it's crucial to acknowledge that these technologies are tools rather than replacements, enhancing rather than replacing the foundational principles of play therapy. The effectiveness of these tools largely depends on their integration into a well-rounded therapeutic plan guided by a skilled therapist.

Looking toward the future implications of these innovations, we must consider factors like accessibility, cost, and training requirements. While promising, the widespread implementation of technologies like VR in play therapy is challenging. The equipment cost and the need for therapists to receive specialized training to use these tools effectively can be significant barriers. However, as technology advances and becomes more integrated into everyday life, these barriers will likely diminish, making these innovative methods more accessible to a broader range of therapists and clients. Furthermore, these technologies' ongoing development and refinement will likely lead to more user-friendly and cost-effective solutions, which could democratize access to cutting-edge therapeutic tools.

Thus, as we continue to explore and integrate these innovative techniques in play therapy, we are enhancing our therapeutic toolkit and paving the way for more personalized, engaging, and effective interventions. These technologies hold the potential to transform the therapeutic landscape, offering new pathways to healing that are aligned with the digital realities of the modern world. As we embrace these changes, we must ensure that they are implemented thoughtfully and ethically, always prioritizing the well-being and development of the children we serve.

8.4 Cross-Cultural Case Studies: Universal Lessons from Diverse Contexts

In a world as varied and vast as ours, play therapy offers a unique window into the universal needs of children, transcending cultural boundaries with the universal language of play. It's in the rich tapestry of global diversity that play therapy finds its true expression, adapting to the nuanced cultural fabrics of children's lives. This adaptability enhances the therapist's ability to connect and communicate and enriches the therapeutic process, making it more effective and resonant for children from many backgrounds.

Cultural sensitivity in therapy is more than an ethical mandate; it's a cornerstone of effective practice. Consider the case of Amina, a young girl from a conservative Middle Eastern background, who was introduced to play therapy to help her cope with severe anxiety and social withdrawal. Her therapist, aware of the cultural emphasis on community and family, incorporated family play into the sessions. This involved Amina's parents and siblings in the therapy through structured family play activities, which made Amina feel supported and respected by her cultural values that emphasize strong family bonds. The therapist used culturally familiar games and storytelling techniques that included tales and characters from Middle Eastern folklore, which Amina found comforting and engaging. This culturally attuned approach allowed Amina to open up more in therapy, facilitating significant progress in her ability to manage anxiety and interact with her peers.

In another instance, the universal therapeutic theme of emotional expression was beautifully illustrated through the play therapy of Juan, a Latino boy who had witnessed domestic violence. His therapist introduced puppet play, which enabled Juan to project his feelings and experiences onto the puppets. This form of play, deeply rooted in the narrative tradition of Latino culture, which values storytelling, allowed Juan to express complex emotions safely and indirectly. The puppets became his voice, narrating stories of fear, anger, resilience, and hope. This not only helped Juan process his traumatic experiences but also reinforced the therapeutic power of play as a tool for emotional exploration and healing.

From these experiences, several vital lessons emerge that can inform and improve play therapy practices globally. First, the importance of cultural competence must be addressed. Therapists must continuously learn about cultural practices and values influencing children's lives. Second, adaptability in therapy techniques to fit cultural contexts shows respect for the child's background and enhances the therapy's relevance and effectiveness. For instance, integrating artistic elements into play, like traditional games or stories, can make the therapeutic process more engaging and meaningful for the child.

Case examples from various cultural contexts further showcase play therapy's global applicability and adaptability. In Japan, therapists use origami, the art of paper folding, as a therapeutic tool to enhance mindfulness and concentration among children with ADHD. In Africa, storytelling and drumming sessions help children express and manage communal and familial tensions experienced in their environments. These examples highlight the versatility of play therapy techniques and underscore the profound impact of culturally resonant practices in enhancing therapeutic outcomes.

As play therapy evolves and adapts across different cultural landscapes, it remains anchored in children's universal needs to express, connect, and heal. This global perspective enriches the practice, offering a broader understanding of the human experience through the playful, resilient eyes of children worldwide.

8.5 Family Play Therapy: Comprehensive Case Examples

In the complex web of family dynamics, where each member plays a pivotal role in the emotional ecosystem, family play therapy emerges as a transformative tool. It addresses the individual's issues and the collective patterns that shape family interactions. Take, for instance, the case of the Thompson family, who entered therapy to address ongoing conflicts between the two siblings, aged 10 and 12, and communication breakdowns with their parents. The family therapist utilized a technique known as family sculpting, allowing each member to position other family members in a physical tableau that represented their perceptions and feelings toward each other. This powerful visual and physical representation illuminated the underlying resentments and alliances within the family, sparking an open dialogue and reshaping their understanding of each other's emotions and perspectives.

This process also revealed significant roles that each family member had unconsciously adopted. The elder sibling felt burdened with expectations as the 'responsible one,' while the younger felt overshadowed and less favored. Through guided play sessions, roles were reversed, and scenarios were enacted where each member could experience and empathize with the other's role, fostering a deeper understanding and appreciation of one another's challenges and contributions to the family. Each family member's involvement was crucial in actively reflecting and working towards changing their interactions. The sessions were designed to encourage expression and negotiation, skills vital for effective communication that needed to be improved.

As the family dynamics unfolded in the therapy room, the success of these interventions became increasingly tied to several critical factors. The level of participation from each family member was paramount; the more involved and engaged they were, the more profound the insights and transformations observed. Openness, another critical factor, where each member was encouraged to express their true feelings without fear of judgment, allowed genuine issues to surface and be addressed.

Lastly, the therapist's skill and sensitivity in navigating the complex emotional landscapes of family interactions played a central role in guiding the family toward healthier ways of relating to one another.

In another application of family play therapy, the Greene family dealt with the fallout of a recent divorce. The integrative technique of group narrative therapy was employed, where the family collaboratively created a story that mirrored their real-life situation but with alternative outcomes. This narrative approach allowed the family members, especially the children, to express their fears and hopes regarding the new family structure. It helped them envision a positive framework for their future interactions. The narrative built was one of cooperation and shared parental responsibilities, which helped alleviate the children's anxieties about the changes in their family life.

The success of the Greene family's therapy hinged on their willingness to engage deeply with the process, their openness to confronting uncomfortable emotions, and the therapist's ability to keep the narrative focused yet flexible enough to accommodate and address each family member's concerns. The therapy sessions provided a safe and creative environment for the family to explore and understand the shifts in their relationships, facilitating a smoother transition into their new life configuration.

Family play therapy, focusing on collective healing and understanding, is a powerful modality in addressing and alleviating the intricate issues that families face. By tailoring sessions to meet each family's specific emotional and relational needs, therapists can facilitate meaningful changes that resonate beyond the therapy room, fostering healthier and more resilient family dynamics. As these case examples show, the efficacy of family play therapy lies in its ability to weave together individual stories into a coherent narrative that supports growth, understanding, and connection among all family members. Through this therapeutic journey, families learn not just to address immediate conflicts but to develop enduring strategies for communication and mutual support, which are essential for navigating the complexities of family life.

8.6 School-Based Play Therapy: Strategies and Successes

In the bustling corridors and classrooms of schools, where academic pressures and social dynamics intermingle, school-based play therapy emerges as a vital resource. It addresses a spectrum of challenges, from bullying and academic stress to difficulties in social integration. These issues, if left unaddressed, can impede a child's educational and social success. By incorporating play therapy within the school environment, we open a therapeutic window that allows students to explore solutions and strategies in a familiar space, thus enhancing the therapy's accessibility and relevance.

Implementing play therapy programs in schools involves a collaborative and structured approach. Sessions are typically integrated into the school day, providing minimal disruption to the student's routine. This integration requires close collaboration with school staff to ensure the therapy aligns with the student's educational goals and the broader school environment. For instance, therapists often work alongside teachers to identify behaviors that may indicate underlying issues such as anxiety or learning difficulties. These observations guide the focus of the play therapy sessions, ensuring they are relevant and targeted. Play therapists might use a dedicated space within the school, such as a quiet room or a corner of the library, to create a safe and inviting play environment. The sessions often mirror the school's schedule, with regular short sessions that help build consistency and trust without overwhelming the students.

The success of these interventions is vividly illustrated through case studies in diverse school settings. One notable example comes from a middle school in a high-needs district, where a significant number of students dealt with aggression and peer conflict. Introducing a play therapy program tailored to address conflict resolution and emotional expression led to noticeable improvements. Through role-playing exercises and group activities, students learned practical ways to express their feelings and resolve disagreements. The school reported a marked reduction in classroom disruptions and bullying incidents, contributing to a more harmonious school environment.

Another compelling case involved a primary school facing high levels of academic stress among students. The play therapy program implemented there focused on stress management techniques, using activities like guided imagery and therapeutic storytelling to help students express their anxieties and fears about academic performance. These playful, creative sessions allowed students to tackle their stress indirectly, making the process less intimidating and more engaging. Teacher feedback suggested improved concentration and reduced anxiety in students, particularly during exams and other high-stress periods.

The feedback from teachers, parents, and students further underscores the effectiveness of school-based play therapy. Teachers often note improvements in student behavior and engagement in the classroom, attributing these changes to the skills and coping mechanisms learned during play therapy. Parents observe a tremendous enthusiasm for school and reduced school-related stress at home. Students report feeling more understood and supported, with many expressing a newfound enjoyment in their school experience. Quantitative and qualitative evaluations, such as behavioral assessments and satisfaction surveys, consistently demonstrate the positive impact of play therapy on students' emotional well-being and academic performance.

These insights highlight the practical benefits of integrating play therapy into school settings and emphasize its role in fostering a supportive educational environment. By addressing emotional and behavioral challenges through play, students are better equipped to face academic pressures and build healthy social relationships. This holistic approach to student well-being is a testament to the versatility and efficacy of play therapy in adapting to and meeting the diverse needs of students across different school environments.

As we reflect on the transformative impacts of school-based play therapy detailed in this chapter, it's clear that the journey of integrating therapeutic play into educational settings is not just beneficial but essential. The case studies and strategies discussed here illuminate a path forward for schools seeking to support their students comprehensively. It's a path that respects the complex interplay of learning, emotional growth, and social interaction in shaping a child's educational experience. As we turn the page to the next chapter, we carry forward the understanding that play therapy, with its unique ability to weave joy and learning into the fabric of therapy, is a powerful ally in the quest for nurturing well-rounded, resilient students.

Chapter 9

Overcoming Challenges in Play Therapy

I n the nuanced dance of play therapy, each step forward can sometimes be met with a step back, especially when resistance forms part of the rhythm. Think of resistance not as a barrier but as a deeply woven thread in the tapestry of therapeutic progress—a cue that there's more beneath the surface to be understood and gently unraveled. This chapter delves into the delicate art of navigating resistance in child clients, a common yet complex challenge that can surface during therapeutic sessions. Understanding the roots of this resistance and adopting strategies to address it gracefully can transform potential obstacles into opportunities for deeper insight and connection.

9.1 Dealing with Resistance in Child Clients

Understanding the Roots of Resistance

Resistance in play therapy can often appear as a refusal to participate in activities, overt skepticism towards the therapy process, or recurring disruptive behaviors. While these responses might seem obstructive, they are, more often than not, manifestations of deeper psychological and environmental factors. Fear, for instance, is a prevalent root of resistance. A child who has experienced instability, trauma, or significant changes might fear the vulnerability that comes with the therapeutic exploration of their emotions. Mistrust, another critical factor, can develop from previous negative experiences with adults or authority figures, leading children to be wary of opening up in a seemingly adult-driven process.

Environmental factors also play a crucial role. Family dynamics, cultural background, or daily peer interactions might influence a child's resistance. For example, a child from a highly private family might be hesitant to express personal feelings, viewing such openness as a breach of familial norms. Additionally, children who are bullied or ostracized may resist participating in activities that expose their vulnerabilities to others for fear of further judgment or rejection.

Recognizing these underlying resistance causes is the first step in addressing them effectively. It requires a therapist to be not just a facilitator of play but a compassionate observer, equipped with an understanding that resistance is not a defiance of therapy but a communication of need.

Strategies to Overcome Resistance

Transforming resistance into engagement is a process that begins with the establishment of trust. Trust can be cultivated through consistent and predictable actions that reassure the child of the safety and reliability of the therapeutic environment. For instance, maintaining a consistent routine for therapy sessions can provide a sense of stability, helping to alleviate anxiety associated with unpredictability. Furthermore, using non-threatening forms of play can invite participation without pressure. Activities that allow parallel play, where the therapist and child play independently but alongside each other, can be particularly effective. This method demonstrates acceptance of the child's pace and comfort level, gradually encouraging more interactive engagement as the child feels safer.

Allowing the child to lead the direction of therapy is another powerful strategy for mitigating resistance. This child-centered approach respects the child's autonomy and acknowledges their role in their healing process. When children choose their activities or direct the play narrative, they gain a sense of control that can break down resistance barriers. For instance, children might be more willing to engage with a puppet show if they are allowed to choose the characters and the storyline rather than being asked to follow a pre-set script that feels alien or imposing.

Interactive Element: Reflective Journal Prompt

Consider a situation where a child shows resistance in a therapy session. Reflect on how you use consistent routines and child-led play to create a safer, more inviting space for them. How could these strategies reduce resistance and deepen the therapeutic impact?

Navigating resistance in play therapy requires patience, empathy, and a deep commitment to understanding the child's worldview. Adopting strategies that build trust, respecting the child's pace, and empowering their sense of control can turn resistance into a gateway for deeper emotional exploration and healing. This approach addresses the immediate challenges of resistance and fosters a therapeutic relationship that can facilitate significant growth and transformation in the child's life.

9.2 Managing Caregiver Expectations and Involvement

In play therapy, the role of caregivers is pivotal, not just as participants but as partners in the therapeutic journey. Educating caregivers about the goals and methods of play therapy is foundational to this partnership. It's crucial for you, as therapists, to articulate clearly what play therapy involves and what it aims to achieve. Often, caregivers come with preconceived notions that play therapy is merely about children playing with toys rather than a structured form of psychotherapy aimed at solving complex emotional and behavioral issues. By holding initial consultations and ongoing educational sessions, you can help caregivers understand that each play activity is carefully chosen to elicit specific therapeutic outcomes and that their child's engagement in seemingly simple play is critical to their emotional and cognitive development.

Setting realistic expectations is another cornerstone of effectively managing caregiver involvement. It's natural for caregivers to want quick resolutions to their child's issues; however, therapeutic change often requires time and patience. Regular discussions about the therapy's progress and what milestones to expect can help recalibrate expectations and reassure caregivers about the efficacy of the process. For instance, explaining that improvements in a child's behavior might initially appear in therapy before they become evident at home or in school can help caregivers set realistic timelines and appreciate subtle progress they might otherwise overlook.

Balancing caregiver involvement with maintaining professional boundaries presents its own set of challenges. While it's beneficial for caregivers to understand and support the therapy process, there must be a clear delineation between their role and yours. Encouraging caregivers to observe sessions through one-way mirrors or to participate in guided play sessions can be effective. Still, it's crucial to communicate that the therapy room allows children to express themselves without fear of direct judgment or discipline from their parents. This helps preserve the integrity of the therapeutic relationship and ensures that therapy remains a safe space for the child. Additionally, setting boundaries regarding communication, such as scheduled updates and feedback sessions, rather than on-demand reporting, respects the therapeutic process and your professional time.

Handling unrealistic or misinformed expectations from caregivers involves a delicate blend of empathy and education. When caregivers expect immediate or specific outcomes, it's essential to realign these expectations with the realities of therapeutic progress gently. This involves discussing the nature of developmental changes, which are often gradual and non-linear, or explaining the child's unique therapeutic needs, which differ from those of other children. Regular updates on the child's progress, accompanied by specific examples of therapeutic achievements, can also help caregivers see the value in the ongoing process. For instance, sharing a story of how a child used a new coping skill learned in therapy during a challenging situation at home can make the therapy's benefits tangible to caregivers.

Facilitating Positive Caregiver Support

Positive caregiver support is integral to the success of play therapy. It not only reinforces the therapeutic techniques used in sessions but also extends the nurturing impact of therapy into the home environment. It is crucial to educate caregivers on how they can support their child's therapeutic journey at home. This might include simple strategies like using similar language to acknowledge feelings or setting up a dedicated 'play time' that mirrors the structure of therapy sessions, allowing children to continue their exploratory and expressive play outside of the therapeutic setting. For instance, if a child uses a specific toy in therapy to express complex emotions, having a similar toy at home could provide continuity and a sense of security.

Workshops or training sessions that teach caregivers play therapy techniques can also be beneficial. These sessions can empower caregivers to engage more productively in their child's emotional development and ensure that the child receives consistent support across all environments. Moreover, these interactions allow caregivers to ask questions and share feedback, enhancing the therapeutic process by giving you insights into the child's behavior in different settings.

Managing caregiver expectations and involvement ultimately aims to foster a collaborative environment where therapists and caregivers work together to support the child's development. By educating, setting boundaries, addressing expectations, and facilitating positive support, you can enhance the efficacy of play therapy and ensure a more holistic support system for each child. This approach maximizes the therapeutic benefits and fosters a deeper understanding and respect between all parties involved, paving the way for more meaningful and sustained developmental progress.

9.3 Overcoming Cultural Barriers in Therapy Sessions

In the tapestry of play therapy, cultural sensitivity is not merely an added skill but a fundamental aspect of providing effective and empathetic care. Recognizing and valuing the diverse backgrounds of the children we serve enriches the therapeutic relationship and enhances the overall effectiveness of the therapy. To this end, ongoing cultural sensitivity training for therapists is crucial. Such training involves more than the occasional workshop or seminar; it is a continuous commitment to understanding the nuanced realities of different cultures, beliefs, and family dynamics that shape the lives of our clients. Engaging in regular training sessions helps keep therapists attuned to the broad spectrum of cultural expressions and issues, ensuring that our therapeutic approaches remain respectful and relevant. These sessions often include learning from cultural experts, participating in community events, and consuming media that offer insights into different cultural experiences. This can deepen a therapist's competence and confidence in addressing cultural nuances within therapy sessions.

Incorporating cultural elements into play therapy sessions is a dynamic way to enhance relatability and effectiveness. When children see their cultures and lifestyles reflected in the therapeutic setting, it validates their identity and strengthens their engagement in therapy. For example, using play materials that represent a child's cultural background—such as dolls that resemble their ethnic features or storybooks that include tales from their heritage—can make the play experience more familiar and comforting. Moreover, celebrating various cultural festivals through 'play' activities can allow children to learn about and appreciate different customs and traditions, fostering a sense of global citizenship and respect. These thoughtful inclusions help bridge the child's world and the therapeutic environment, making therapy a more inclusive and affirming space.

Navigating language differences is another significant aspect of cultural sensitivity in play therapy. Language barriers can hinder a child's ability to express themselves fully and benefit from therapy. To overcome this, therapists might employ translation services or bilingual staff, ensuring that communication remains clear and compelling. Additionally, using culturally familiar symbols and non-verbal forms of communication, such as music or art from the child's culture, can significantly enhance understanding. These adaptations require therapists to be flexible and creative in their approach, often tailoring sessions to meet each child's specific linguistic and cultural needs. This not only aids in effective communication but also demonstrates a deep respect for the child's background, which can significantly strengthen the therapeutic bond.

Building trust within diverse communities involves proactive outreach and genuine collaboration with community leaders and groups. This can be particularly impactful in communities where there might be skepticism about mental health practices or where previous negative experiences have created barriers to accessing therapy. Therapists can foster trust and cooperation by engaging with community leaders, attending community events, and providing educational workshops about the benefits of play therapy. These efforts help demystify the therapy process for communities, making it more accessible and acceptable. Furthermore, involving community members in developing culturally sensitive therapy practices can provide invaluable insights that enhance the therapy's relevance and effectiveness. This collaborative approach enriches the therapist's understanding and connection with different cultures and builds a foundation of mutual respect and trust that is crucial for effective therapy.

Navigating the complexities of cultural diversity requires a commitment to continuous learning, respect for individual experiences, and an adaptable approach to therapy. By embracing these practices, therapists overcome cultural barriers and enrich their professional and personal growth, leading to more meaningful and effective therapeutic encounters.

9.4 Documentation and Measuring Progress in Play Therapy

In the nuanced realm of play therapy, the significance of meticulous and precise documentation cannot be overstated. It functions much like a compass, guiding the therapeutic journey—it helps evaluate the child's progress, shapes future therapy sessions, and ensures a structured approach to emotional and behavioral development. Thorough documentation captures the subtleties and shifts in the child's interactions and behaviors during play, providing a reliable basis for assessing therapeutic outcomes and planning subsequent interventions. Each session's detailed records become a chapter in a broader story of a child's journey through therapy, offering invaluable insights into their developmental strides and challenges.

Effective documentation practices hinge on consistency and detail. It's crucial to record what activities were performed, how the child engaged with them, their responses to different scenarios, and any significant statements or emotional expressions they made. This might include noting down a child's facial expressions, non-verbal cues, and interactions with toys and peers during a session. Such comprehensive records help create a multidimensional view of the child's therapeutic progress and are essential for tailoring future sessions to meet their evolving needs better.

Embracing digital tools for organizing and securing documentation can enhance the efficiency and accuracy of this process. Digital recording tools, for example, can be used to capture real-time notes and audio recordings during sessions, which can be particularly useful for capturing nuances that might otherwise be missed in handwritten notes. Secure digital databases offer robust platforms for storing sensitive information, ensuring that each child's records are kept confidential and are easily accessible for review by authorized personnel. These digital systems often come with features that allow for the categorization and quick retrieval of information, making it easier to track a child's progress over time and across various parameters.

Measuring Therapy Progress

The measurement of play therapy's progress integrates qualitative and quantitative approaches, providing a holistic view of the child's developmental journey. Behavioral observations during sessions are pivotal; they involve looking at how a child's responses and interactions evolve over time. For instance, decreasing aggressive outbursts or increasing cooperative play can be significant progress indicators. When consistently documented, these observations paint a picture of gradual change that might not be as perceptible daily.

Feedback from caregivers and teachers is also critical to measuring therapy outcomes. These stakeholders can provide external perspectives on the child's behavior in different environments, such as home or school, offering insights that might not be directly observable during therapy sessions. For example, a teacher might note that a child has started participating more in class or seems less anxious during tests and presentations. When aligned with therapy goals, such feedback can significantly validate the therapeutic interventions' effectiveness.

Self-reports from the child, where appropriate, also offer direct insights into their perceptions of their changes and challenges. Older children, in particular, can provide valuable first-person perspectives on what they feel has improved and what areas they find challenging. These self-assessments encourage self-awareness and active participation in therapy, empowering children as collaborators in their developmental journey.

Using Documentation in Supervision and Consultation

The strategic use of documentation extends beyond the immediate therapeutic setting—it plays a crucial role in supervision and consultation, helping improve therapy practices and outcomes. In supervisory settings, detailed session notes can facilitate nuanced discussions about case management strategies, therapist-client dynamics, and intervention effectiveness. These discussions often lead to enhanced therapeutic techniques and refined intervention strategies, ultimately improving client outcomes. For instance, a supervisor might review documented sessions and suggest alternative approaches or new activities to address specific behavioral patterns more effectively.

In peer consultations, sharing and discussing different cases with detailed documentation can broaden a therapist's understanding of various therapeutic approaches and client interactions. This collaborative learning environment can spark new ideas, highlight potential areas for improvement, and reinforce effective practices across different cases. It also helps build a supportive professional community that values continuous learning and mutual support, which are essential for long-term success in play therapy.

As you continue to navigate the complexities of play therapy, remember that each note you take, observation you record, and piece of feedback you incorporate add depth and effectiveness to your therapeutic practice. Through these meticulous efforts, therapy can truly respond to each child's unique needs, facilitating a journey of meaningful growth and profound healing.

9.5 Refreshing Burnt Out Therapists through Creative Play

In the demanding world of play therapy, where practitioners pour their energy and empathy into fostering growth and healing, it's not uncommon to encounter the shadow of burnout. This condition, characterized by decreased motivation, emotional exhaustion, and reduced job satisfaction, can subtly creep into your daily routine, dimming the vibrancy with which you approach your practice. Recognizing these signs early on is crucial. You might notice a persistent feeling of fatigue, detachment from your work, or decreased satisfaction from achievements that once brought joy. These are not just fleeting moments of tiredness but signs that you are operating without replenishing your emotional and creative reserves.

Addressing burnout proactively involves a commitment to self-care, explicitly focusing on integrating creative play into your life. As therapists, you routinely facilitate play to unlock emotional expression and creativity in children, yet often neglect to apply the same principles to yourselves. Engaging in creative play isn't merely an act of leisure; it's a form of self-preservation and rejuvenation. This could mean setting aside time for activities that ignite your imagination and passion—perhaps revisiting an old hobby like painting or music or exploring new creative outlets such as dance or creative writing. These activities do more than fill leisure time; they revive your spirit, enhance your well-being, and reignite the passion that drew you to play therapy.

Incorporating these creative activities into your professional routine can significantly enhance your therapeutic practice. It's about bringing creativity and playfulness into your interactions with clients, which can help maintain a fresh perspective and high levels of empathy. Techniques include using therapeutic metaphors during sessions, which requires a creative formulation of expressions that resonate with children, or redesigning your therapy space periodically to reflect themes invigorating both for you and your clients. This continuous infusion of creativity keeps the therapeutic environment dynamic and engaging for the children and you as a practitioner.

Support systems play an indispensable role in managing and preventing burnout. This includes access to professional counseling services, which can provide a space to process your work's emotional demands. Additionally, peer support groups offer a platform to share experiences and strategies for coping with the profession's challenges. These groups can be precious, providing both support and validation from those who understand the unique stresses of your role. Attending regular meetings, whether virtual or in person, can reinforce a sense of community and shared purpose, reminding you that you are not alone in your experiences.

Furthermore, professional resources such as workshops focused on therapist self-care and managing burnout can equip you with practical tools and knowledge to safeguard your well-being. These resources often emphasize the importance of setting clear boundaries between work and personal life, recognizing the signs of emotional fatigue, and developing strategies to ensure a sustainable practice. Engaging with these resources helps you manage burnout and models healthful practices to the families and children you support, reinforcing the importance of mental health and self-care.

In navigating the complexities of play therapy, where you invest deeply in the emotional and developmental journeys of others, remember to invest equally in your journey. By recognizing the signs of burnout, engaging in creative self-care, incorporating rejuvenating activities into your practice, and utilizing support systems, you ensure that your work continues to be a source of fulfillment and growth. This holistic approach enhances your resilience and enriches your capacity to foster resilience in others, making each therapeutic encounter a shared journey of discovery and renewal.

As we conclude this exploration into overcoming challenges in play therapy, remember that a therapist's journey is one of continuous learning, not only about the clients we serve but also about ourselves. Each experience chapter offers insights that enhance our ability to connect, heal, and inspire. As we turn the page to the next chapter, we carry forward the lessons learned, ready to embrace new challenges with renewed vigor and a strengthened spirit.

Chapter 10

Implementing Play Therapy Techniques Effectively

I n the ever-evolving field of play therapy, staying at the forefront of educational advancements and therapeutic innovation isn't just beneficial—it's essential. As you continue to guide children through the intricate dance of growth and healing, the need for continuous professional development becomes apparent. This chapter delves into the myriad of resources and avenues available to you, aiming to enrich your practice and ensure your approaches remain fresh, effective, and aligned with the latest research. Whether you are new to the field or looking to deepen your expertise, the learning journey never truly ends, and each step you take enriches your professional life and the lives of those you touch.

10.1 Training and Resources for Play Therapists: Continuing Education and Support

The Importance of Continuing Education

In the dynamic realm of play therapy, where new techniques and theoretical approaches continuously reshape our understanding and practices, the necessity of ongoing education cannot be overstated. Engaging in continuous learning is crucial for keeping up with the evolving landscape of therapeutic strategies and deepening your understanding of children's complex psychological and emotional needs. It ensures that your methods are effective and infused with empathy, creativity, and respect for the diverse backgrounds of the children you support. This ongoing educational journey also reinforces adherence to ethical practices, providing you with the tools to navigate the challenges that often arise in therapeutic settings.

Recommended Training Programs

Navigating the vast seas of available training programs and certifications can be daunting. Yet, selecting the right educational opportunities is pivotal for enhancing your skills and ensuring your approaches are rooted in proven effective methods. The Association for Play Therapy (APT) offers a structured pathway to becoming a Registered Play Therapist (RPT). This designation not only enriches your understanding but also elevates your professional credibility. Additionally, institutions like the Play Therapy Training Institute provide various workshops and courses covering everything from basic techniques to advanced interventions for specific disorders. Online platforms such as the Theraplay Institute offer flexibility with webinars and online courses that focus on attachment-based play therapy, which is ideal for accommodating the busy schedules of working professionals. Each program is designed to challenge your perceptions and expand your skill set, ensuring your practice remains at the cutting edge of therapeutic advancements.

Professional Organizations and Journals

Engaging with professional organizations is not merely about networking but immersing yourself in a community dedicated to growth, excellence, and ethical practices. The Association for Play Therapy provides certification and hosts annual conferences and local chapter meetings that present opportunities to learn from leading experts in the field. Membership offers access to a wealth of resources, including the "International Journal of Play Therapy," a peer-reviewed publication that delves into the latest research and clinical practices, offering insights and case studies that can directly inform and improve your therapeutic techniques.

Peer Learning and Supervision

The value of peer consultation groups and supervision in play therapy cannot be overstated. Engaging regularly with peers provides a platform to share experiences, seek advice on complex cases, and receive support in navigating professional challenges. Finding a mentor for supervision, particularly when tackling more challenging therapeutic scenarios or venturing into new areas of play therapy, can provide you with insights and guidance crucial for professional growth and maintaining therapeutic integrity. These relationships foster a collaborative learning environment where shared knowledge enhances individual practice and contributes to the broader field of play therapy.

Interactive Element: Reflective Journal Prompt

Consider your current engagement with professional development in play therapy. Reflect on the last learning activity you participated in—a workshop, seminar, or journal article. How has this experience influenced your current practice? What new insights did you gain, and how have you integrated these into your therapeutic approach?

This reflection reinforces your learning and encourages a proactive stance in your professional development journey.

By embracing these educational opportunities and resources, you ensure your practice reflects current standards and is a beacon of innovation and deep, empathetic understanding. Each child you encounter in your therapy room benefits from your commitment to learning and refining your craft, making each session a stepping stone to better mental health and emotional resilience.

10.2 Measuring Success in Play Therapy: Tools and Techniques for Evaluation

As you refine your craft in play therapy, understanding the impact of your interventions is crucial. Measuring success in play therapy isn't just about noting observable changes; it involves a nuanced approach that considers behavioral shifts, psychological development, and the subjective well-being of your young clients. Success can manifest in various forms—perhaps a child who once struggled to express their emotions now talks about their feelings freely, or another who had difficulties with peer relationships begins to form friendships. These transformations are the milestones that mark the effectiveness of your therapeutic interventions. Additionally, psychological assessments can provide quantifiable data on a child's progress, offering insights invaluable for current treatment strategies and future therapeutic planning. Self-reported improvements by older children, who can articulate their feelings and experiences more directly, also serve as a significant indicator of the therapy's impact.

Various tools are at your disposal to systematically evaluate the progress and successes of your sessions. Observational checklists serve as one of the primary tools, allowing you to record specific behaviors and responses during sessions. These checklists can be tailored to track the developmental goals set for each child, providing a structured way to monitor changes over time. Standardized tests, such as the Child Behavior Checklist, offer another layer of evaluation, giving standardized data that can help compare a child's outcomes against normative data. Moreover, client feedback forms filled out by parents or caregivers can offer another perspective on a child's behavior outside of therapy sessions. Shed light on changes that might not be directly observable during sessions but are evident in everyday interactions and behaviors at home or school.

Regular feedback sessions with the child and their family is another cornerstone of effective play therapy. These discussions are invaluable as they allow you to gauge satisfaction and gather insights about the child's feelings towards the therapy and any noticeable changes they perceive daily. Structuring these discussions can vary; however, maintaining a consistent format can help children and families feel more comfortable and open in sharing their thoughts. Open-ended questions like "What did you enjoy most about today's session?" or "Have you noticed any changes in how you feel or act at home or school?" can encourage more detailed responses. Using drawings or story-telling to express their feelings about the therapy sessions can be more effective for younger children than direct questions.

Lastly, the continuous improvement of your therapy approach is essential. Using the data gathered from tools and feedback, you should regularly assess the effectiveness of your techniques and make necessary adjustments to your therapy plans. This may mean introducing new activities that align better with the child's evolving interests or therapeutic needs or scaling back on specific interventions that might not be as effective as anticipated. This iterative process ensures that your therapy methods remain aligned with the best outcomes for each child and contributes to the larger field of play therapy by refining what works best in varied contexts.

This dynamic approach to measuring success in play therapy emphasizes the importance of being responsive and adaptive, qualities that define not just a good therapist but a great one who truly sees and responds to the needs of each child. As you continue to utilize these tools and techniques, remember that each piece of feedback and every bit of data you gather serves a larger purpose—it helps tailor a therapeutic environment that is both nurturing and effective, paving the way for meaningful change in the lives of the children you work with.

10.3 Tailoring Play Therapy to Individual Child Profiles: Personalization Tips

When you step into play therapy, each child you meet brings a unique set of experiences, needs, and personalities into the therapeutic space. Understanding and embracing this individuality is crucial, as it forms the foundation for effective and impactful therapy. Initial assessment techniques are your first tools for crafting a therapy approach that speaks directly to each child's situation.

These techniques range from structured interviews with the child and their caregivers, where you gather detailed background information and observe the child's behavior, to play-based assessments that allow you to see the child in action. These assessments involve setting up a miniature world and observing how the child interacts with it, which can reveal insights into their problem-solving skills, emotional states, and social interactions. Collaborating with other professionals such as teachers, pediatricians, or other therapists who have worked with the child can also provide a more comprehensive view of the child's needs and behaviors, ensuring that your approach is well-rounded and informed.

Customizing play activities to suit each child's unique profile is not just about changing the type of toys or games used in sessions; it's about aligning the therapeutic process with the child's cultural background, interests, and specific emotional or behavioral challenges. This customization makes therapy engaging and relevant for the child. For instance, if you're working with a child interested in outer space, incorporating stories or play scenarios that involve astronauts and space missions can make sessions more captivating and compelling. Similarly, understanding and integrating elements from a child's cultural background can make them feel respected and understood, such as using folk tales from their culture as part of storytelling therapy or incorporating traditional games. Furthermore, for children facing specific emotional challenges like anxiety, activities that promote relaxation and sensory soothing, such as water play or sand therapy, can be particularly beneficial.

Involving children in their therapy planning is profoundly empowering. It gives them a sense of control and agency over their therapy journey, which can be particularly important for children who may feel they have little control over other areas of their lives. This involvement can be as simple as allowing them to choose which activities to start with each session or having them help set up the play area. For older children, it might involve discussing the goals of therapy and brainstorming together on the types of activities they believe would be helpful. This collaborative approach ensures that the activities are engaging and relevant. It enhances the therapeutic alliance between you and the child, as they feel heard and valued in their therapy process.

Flexibility and adaptability are some of the most critical attributes you can cultivate as a play therapist. Children's responses to therapy can be highly variable, and what works one day might not work the next. Being ready to shift tactics or approaches based on the child's mood, reactions, or feedback during a session is critical. This might mean changing a planned activity midway through a session if it's not engaging the child or causing distress. It also involves being open to verbal and non-verbal feedback from the child about what they find helpful or enjoyable. This adaptive approach ensures that each session is productive and models a flexible and responsive way of interacting with the world for the child, which is a valuable life skill.

By focusing on these aspects of personalization in play therapy, you create a therapeutic environment that respects and responds to each child's individuality, paving the way for more effective and meaningful therapeutic outcomes. Through careful assessment, thoughtful customization, collaborative planning, and flexible adaptation, you build a therapy practice that meets children where they are, helping them move toward healing and growth in a supportive, safe, and advantageous way.

10.4 Overcoming Resistance in Play Therapy: Strategies for Engagement

Resistance in play therapy is common, and understanding its roots is the first step toward effective engagement. Children might resist participation due to fear, mistrust, or simply misunderstanding what therapy entails. Fear often stems from past negative experiences, perhaps with adults or settings that felt unsafe or unfamiliar. Mistrust might be linked to these experiences or could arise from the child's general apprehension toward new adults, especially if their relationships have historically been unstable. Misunderstandings about therapy can occur if the child feels that the sessions might be another arena where they must meet certain expectations or are being 'tested' in some way. Recognizing these underlying causes is crucial for tailoring your approach to effectively meet the child's emotional and psychological needs.

Engaging a child who shows resistance requires patience, creativity, and a deep understanding of what might motivate them. One effective technique is incorporating their preferred play items into the session. For instance, if a child is particularly fond of dinosaurs, integrating dinosaur figures into the play might help them feel more at ease and interested. Gradually introducing therapeutic elements allows the child to acclimate to the therapy process at their own pace, reducing overwhelming feelings. Ensuring the environment feels non-threatening is also vital. This might mean arranging the therapy room to be more open and inviting, using soft lighting, or letting the child choose where to sit, all of which can contribute to a sense of safety and control for the child.

Building trust and rapport with resistant clients is a gradual process that flourishes with consistency and genuine care. Every interaction with the child is an opportunity to reinforce trust. This can be done through consistent positive interactions where the child feels heard and valued. Respecting the child's pace is crucial; pushing too hard or too fast can reinforce resistance rather than alleviate it. Demonstrating unconditional acceptance helps the child understand that the therapy space is a non-judgmental environment where they can express themselves without fear of criticism or rejection. Such an environment encourages them to engage more openly over time.

Parental Involvement in Overcoming Resistance

The role of parents in managing resistance is indispensable. They are often the most consistent figures in a child's life and can provide reassurance and encouragement towards engaging in therapy. The first step is educating parents about the nature of resistance and the importance of play therapy. Explain that resistance is a normal reaction and can be diminished with time and the right approach. Encouraging parents to speak positively about therapy sessions at home, emphasizing fun and exciting activities rather than framing them as medical or corrective measures, can also change the child's perception of what therapy involves.

Strategies for parents include accompanying the child to sessions and gradually reducing their presence as the child becomes more comfortable. For some children, knowing a parent is close by can provide the security they need to engage with the therapist. Parents can also reinforce the value of therapy by discussing any positive changes they notice at home, linking these improvements to the child's participation in therapy. This makes the sessions more relevant to the child and highlights the tangible benefits of their involvement.

In summary, overcoming resistance in play therapy hinges on a deep understanding of the child's fears and needs, thoughtful use of engagement techniques, and strategic involvement of parents. By creating a therapy environment that feels safe, inclusive, and responsive to the child's pace, you pave the way for more effective and meaningful therapeutic interactions. As you continue to navigate these challenges, remember that each small breakthrough contributes significantly to the overall well-being and growth of the child in your care.

10.5 Future Trends in Play Therapy: What's Next for Practitioners?

In play therapy, the horizon constantly evolves with innovations and adaptations that promise to enhance how we connect with and heal our young clients. As you navigate the future landscapes of this field, understanding and integrating emerging techniques and tools become crucial. The recent surge in digital tools, including virtual reality (VR) applications and advanced therapeutic software, offers unprecedented ways to engage children in therapeutic scenarios that were once confined to the imagination. Imagine a session where a child, through VR, can conquer fears by facing virtual scenarios in a controlled and safe environment or where apps that track emotional responses help tailor sessions in real-time to suit the child's emotional state.

The potential for these technologies in play therapy is vast. VR, for instance, can simulate social situations for children struggling with social anxiety, providing them with practice and confidence in a safe setting before they face real-world scenarios. Additionally, new therapeutic models that integrate these technologies are being developed, offering therapists frameworks to include these tools effectively in their practice. However, as you incorporate these advanced tools, staying grounded in the core principles of play therapy—empathy, creativity, and child-centered approaches—remains essential.

Staying abreast of current research is another pillar crucial to the evolution of your practice. The landscape of play therapy research is rich with ongoing studies that validate the effectiveness of traditional techniques and explore the potential of new methods. Engaging with this research informs your practice and contributes to the broader knowledge base by sharing your observations and outcomes. Journals and periodicals dedicated to psychological therapies and child development are invaluable resources, offering insights into the latest findings and discussions in the field. Engaging with this literature can spark ideas for adapting your methods or trying new approaches based on the latest evidence-based practices.

Looking at play therapy through a global lens reveals the increasing importance of cultural adaptability in therapeutic practices. As our societies become more interconnected, the children we serve come from increasingly diverse backgrounds. This diversity requires that our therapeutic approaches be adaptable to various cultural contexts. It's about more than just translating existing practices into different languages or incorporating culturally specific items into the playroom. It involves a deep understanding and respect for cultural nuances that influence how children perceive and interact with the world. International collaboration and learning are beneficial, allowing you to gain insights into how play therapy is practiced in different parts of the world and integrating these learnings to enhance your practice. Such collaborations can occur through international conferences, joint research projects, or peer connections facilitated by global professional organizations.

Ethical considerations, particularly about the use of technology, are becoming increasingly complex. As digital tools become more integrated into play therapy, data privacy, consent, and the potential for over-reliance on technology need careful consideration. The therapeutic space of confidentiality and trust must be upheld even as we use more digital methods. Furthermore, maintaining professional boundaries becomes more challenging yet crucial as we navigate therapy in increasingly diverse settings. Adhering to ethical guidelines set forth by professional bodies and participating in ongoing ethics training helps safeguard the interests and well-being of the children we serve.

As you step into the future of play therapy, equipped with new tools and informed by a wealth of global research and perspectives, remember that at the heart of your practice is the well-being of each child. Each innovation or new knowledge is a potential key to unlocking more profound understanding and connection, helping you guide your young clients toward healing and growth in an ever-changing world.

10.6 Creating a Play Therapy Toolkit: Must-Have Items for Effective Practice

In the dynamic practice of play therapy, your toolkit is your foundation and creative palette. It comprises a variety of toys, art supplies, games, and digital resources, each serving a specific therapeutic purpose. Think of this toolkit not just as a collection of items but as a curated selection that you can draw upon to meet the unique needs of each child you work with. These tools are extensions of your therapeutic intent, mediums through which you can facilitate expression, exploration, and healing.

Essential Tools and Materials

At the core of any play therapist's toolkit are the toys, which should be as diverse as the children you serve. These essential tools and materials range from simple, tactile objects like playdough and sand, which can be soothing and provide a medium for expression, to more complex items like dolls and action figures that help children act out social scenarios and explore different roles. Art supplies such as markers, crayons, and paper are indispensable for art therapy interventions, allowing children to express feelings and thoughts that might be too complex to articulate verbally. Board games and puzzles encourage cognitive development and problem-solving skills and facilitate social interaction and learning turn-taking and rule-following. Each tool has its place, helping unlock the voices of children who might struggle to communicate their internal experiences.

Digital Resources

In today's digital age, incorporating technology into your play therapy sessions can enhance traditional techniques and offer new pathways for engagement. Digital tools such as tablets can access therapeutic apps or display soothing scenes and sounds that help create a calming environment. Apps that facilitate drawing or storytelling allow for creative expressions that are easily saved and revisited, providing a digital footprint of a child's progress. However, using digital tools should always complement, rather than replace, the hands-on elements of play therapy. They should be chosen with care, ensuring they are appropriate for the child's age and developmental stage and used in a way that enhances the therapeutic goals rather than distracting from them.

Documentation and Record Keeping

Maintaining detailed records is crucial in play therapy. Not only do these records help track a child's progress over time, but they also provide invaluable insights into the effectiveness of your interventions. Utilizing digital systems can streamline this process, allowing you to keep comprehensive notes that are easily accessible and securely stored. Software designed for therapeutic practices can enable you to annotate session notes with observations and to link these notes to specific therapeutic goals and outcomes. Moreover, video recording sessions, with the appropriate consent, can be an excellent tool for review and supervision, allowing you to observe nuances that might have been missed in the moment.

Self-Care Resources

Finally, it's vital to include self-care resources in your toolkit. The emotional demands of play therapy can be considerable, and maintaining your well-being is essential to providing the best care for your clients. This might include access to professional support networks or regular supervision where you can process your experiences and receive guidance. Personal self-care tools such as mindfulness apps, reflective practice journals, and physical wellness resources (like yoga or exercise routines) are also essential. These resources help ensure that you are at your best, professionally and personally, as you engage in the significant work of play therapy.

With your toolkit well-assembled and thoughtfully maintained, you are equipped with a collection of items and a robust suite of resources tailored to meet the complex needs of the children you support. This toolkit enhances your capacity to deliver effective therapy and enriches the therapeutic journey for you and your clients.

As this chapter closes, remember that the items in your toolkit are more than just tools; they are bridges to understanding, vehicles for healing, and instruments of change. They empower you to meet each child in their world, join them in their experience, and guide them toward greater resilience and wellness. Let compassion, creativity, and continuous learning lead your choices and enrich your practice as you move forward.

Conclusion

As we conclude our exploration into the transformative power of play therapy, it's essential to reflect on the profound impact this therapeutic intervention can have on children's emotional, social, and developmental well-being. Through the diverse stories and strategies shared in this book, we've seen that play therapy is far more than a set of activities; it is a profoundly impactful practice that nurtures healing and growth in young minds.

Understanding and applying the foundational concepts of play therapy, such as the therapeutic powers of play, the significance of a well-prepared environment, and the critical role of the therapist as a guide and supporter, are pivotal. These elements create a scaffold for effective therapy, ensuring that each session is a time for play and a strategic, meaningful progression toward healing and development.

We've also discussed play therapy's versatility and adaptability, emphasizing that its techniques can be customized for individual needs. This adaptability makes play therapy a universally applicable tool, effective across various settings and populations, including children with diverse backgrounds and challenges. Play therapy can transform lives in schools, clinics, or homes.

The journey is ever-evolving for those who practice play therapy, continually learn, and adapt to new research and ethical considerations. The field of play therapy is dynamic, with new techniques and insights constantly emerging. It's our responsibility to remain engaged in ongoing education and professional development to ensure our practices not only meet the current standards but also push the boundaries of what we can achieve in therapeutic settings.

This book urges all therapists, caregivers, and educators to embrace and integrate cultural sensitivity into their practice. We must foster inclusive and culturally competent practices to ensure that play therapy remains accessible and effective for all children, regardless of their cultural background. By doing so, we uphold a collective responsibility toward creating a nurturing environment that respects and celebrates diversity.

I call upon you, the readers, to apply the insights and strategies discussed to make a tangible difference in the lives of children. View yourselves as crucial contributors to their growth and healing through play. Trust in the process and the substantial evidence base supporting play therapy as a best practice in child therapy. Remember, your involvement does not just benefit the children; it enriches your lives, too, offering a profound sense of accomplishment and joy in witnessing the positive changes you help bring about.

Play therapy is part of a broader support ecosystem for children, including families, schools, and communities. Collaboration and communication among all stakeholders are essential to maximize the therapeutic outcomes and ensure that each child receives the holistic support they need.

This book stands as a comprehensive guide, offering innovative and practical guidance for implementing effective play therapy techniques. It is designed to be an indispensable resource for anyone working with or caring for children, providing foundational knowledge and advanced insights.

In closing, let us move forward with hope and empowerment, motivated by the transformative potential of play therapy. This journey is not just about the children we help; it is also about our growth as compassionate, skilled practitioners who have the privilege of contributing to the developmental milestones of future generations. Let's continue to learn, adapt, and innovate, ensuring we provide the best possible support to the children who depend on us. Together, we can make a lasting difference, one child at a time.

Bonus Worksheets

https://drive.google.com/file/d/1U_V-
JnQFvvfFr73ZuKJXQiZDx6RM_L2k/view?usp=sharing

PLAY THERAPY
WORKSHEETS

Worksheets based on play therapy
practices curated specifically for children
ages 3 to 7 years

FEELINGS FACES

Objective: Help children recognize and name different emotions.
Instructions: Can you color the face that looks like how you feel right now?

Caregiver notes:
  1. Ask the child why they are feeling a certain way.
  2. Encourage them to ask you about your emotions and feelings too.
  3. Tell them what emotion each face represents to help them develop a better sense of emotions and facial expressions.

MY SAFE PLACE

Objective: Help children create a safe space in their mind through drawing.

Instructions: What would your safe place look like? Who would be there with you? Which things would be there? Draw the people and things which make you feel safe in the room and use your favorite colors to bring life to your safe place.

Caregiver notes:

1. Practice mindful breathing with the child before starting this activity.
2. Ask the child about why these certain things and specific people make them feel safe.

EMOTION BINGO

Objective: Encourage children to identify different emotions.
Instructions: Can you find all the feelings in your day? Color the face
each time you feel one!

Caregiver notes:
   1.Ask the child which feeling they experienced the most.
   2.Ask them the reason behind it.
   3.If it a concerning and negative feeling help them work through it
      and feel better.

PLAY THERAPY
WORKSHEETS

Worksheets based on play therapy
practices curated specifically for children
ages 8 to 12 years

FEELINGS IDENTIFICATION AND EXPRESSION

Objective: Help children recognize and express their emotions.
Instructions: Below are some facial expressions. Next to each face,
write about a time you felt that way.

Caregiver notes:
- Take time to discuss what the child expressed and ask guiding
  questions to help them explore their emotions.

MY SAFE SPACE COLORING PAGE

Objective: Help children create their own mental safe space.
Instructions: Below is a simple room. Color and add details to show what your safe place would look like.

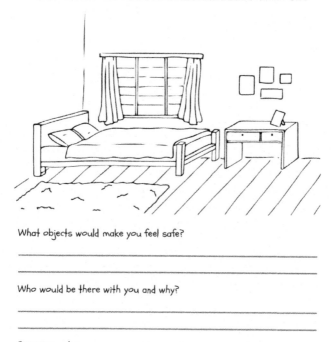

What objects would make you feel safe?

_____

_____

Who would be there with you and why?

_____

_____

Caregiver notes:
- Discuss why the child chose those objects or people and how they can use this visualization to calm down when feeling anxious.
- You may practice mindful breathing with the child before this activity.

WHAT WOULD YOU DO? 1

Objective: Strengthen empathy and social problem-solving.
Instructions: Read the scenario below and think about how you would help your friend. Then, answer the questions and role-play with a caregiver.

Scenario:
Your friend is sitting alone during recess, and they look sad. You know they feel left out because no one invited them to play. What could you say or do to make them feel better?

What is the first thing you would say to your friend?

_____

_____

How do you think your friend might feel after you talk to them?

_____

_____

What are some activities you could invite them to join?

_____

_____

How would you feel if you were in their place?

_____

_____

Caregiver notes:
- Role-play this scenario with the child, discussing different approaches to helping a friend. Ask guiding questions about empathy and how to be a good friend.
- Help them with reading and understanding the scenario and questions, if needed.

Help Others Benefit from Their Innate Need to Play!

"Those who play rarely become brittle in the face of stress or lose the healing capacity for humor." — Stuart Brown, MD

They say that inside every adult is a child who wants to play, and within this simple thought lies the secret of why play therapy is so effective for children. Do you remember the first time a little sibling shared their favorite toy with you, or the time your parents brought home your first boardgame? How about when that math class turned into a hive of learning when the teacher transformed the hour into a fun group game? There is something so primal in our need to play, and this need is felt throughout our lifetime... but above all when we are children.

Throughout your reading journey thus far, you have seen that one of the most powerful reasons why play therapy is so effective is that it is self-directed. When taking part in a play therapy session, kids are freed from feeling like they have to play for a reward or "to win." Instead, the joy lies in the doing, in simply being in a creative and happy state alongside others. Of course, the power of play goes way beyond enjoyment. You have seen how play can be used to strengthen the child-caregiver bond, boost a child's self-esteem, and correct specific behaviors. If you have found the strategies shared thus far to be empowering for both you and the children you are working with, I hope I can ask for a small favor. Please share your thoughts with others, so they, too, can find the information they seek to harness the power of play.

By leaving a review of this book on Amazon, you'll empower new readers to reshape a young life profoundly by teaching kids how to overcome emotional and behavioral challenges through play.

Thanks for your support. Here's to many more fulfilling sessions that tap into the powerful therapeutic benefits of play.

Leave Your Review Today!

References

ChildsWork. (n.d.). The history of play therapy. https://childswork.com/blogs/childswork-childsplay-blog/the history-of-play-therapy

Leong, F. T. L., & Kalibatseva, Z. (2011). Cultural diversity and mental health: Considerations for ... National Center for Biotechnology Information. https://www.ncbi.nlm.nih.gov/pmc/articles/PMC6018386/

Wikipedia contributors. (2023, May 18). Virginia Axline. In Wikipedia, The Free Encyclopedia. https://en.wikipedia.org/wiki/Virginia_Axline

Becoming Me Play Therapy. (n.d.). Digital play therapy. https://www.becomingmeplaytherapy.com.au/digital-play-therapy

Levine, M., & Mihalopoulos, C. (2023). An overview of play therapy. National Center for Biotechnology Information. https://www.ncbi.nlm.nih.gov/pmc/articles/PMC8812369/

Mayo Clinic Staff. (2023). Screen time and children: How to guide your child. Mayo Clinic. https://www.mayoclinic.org/healthy-lifestyle/childrens-health/in-depth/screen-time/art-20047952

Mellenthin, C. (n.d.). Attachment centered play therapy for attachment disorders. https://clairmellenthin.com/powerful-play-therapy-techniques-for-the-treatment-of-childhood-disorders/

Exchange Family Center. (2018, April 10). Connecting with your child through play: The surprising benefits of parent-child playtime. https://www.exchangefamilycenter.org/exchange-family-center-blog/2018/4/10/connecting-with-your-child-through-play-the-surprising-benefits-of-parent-child-playtime

Association for Play Therapy. (n.d.). Play therapy makes a difference. https://www.a4pt.org/page/PTMakesADifference/Play-Therapy-Makes-a-Difference.htm

Positive Psychology. (n.d.). 25 fun mindfulness activities for children & teens (+tips!). https://positivepsychology.com/mindfulness-for-children-kids-activities/

Positive Action. (n.d.). 20 evidence-based social skills activities and games for kids. https://www.positiveaction.net/blog/social-skills-activities-and-games-for-kids

Copeland, J. (n.d.). Art as a tool for emotional expression: Fostering creativity. Coping Skills for Kids. https://copingskillsforkids.com/blog/art-as-emotional-expression

Morin, A. (2023). Play therapy: Definition, types, techniques. Verywell Mind. https://www.verywellmind.com/play-therapy-definition-types-techniques-5194915

Proud to be Primary. (n.d.). Conflict resolution activities: Effective ideas for classrooms. https://proudtobeprimary.com/conflict-resolution-activities/

Morin, A. (2023). *Create a token economy system to improve child behavior. Verywell Family.* https://www.verywellfamily.com/create-a-token-economy-system-to-improve-child-behavior-1094888

National Center for Biotechnology Information. (2023). *Play-based interventions for mental health: A systematic review.* https://www.ncbi.nlm.nih.gov/pmc/articles/PMC9685160/

National Center for Biotechnology Information. (2023). *Play therapy in children with autism: Its role, implications, and benefits.* https://www.ncbi.nlm.nih.gov/pmc/articles/PMC9850869/

Ray, D. C., Ogawa, Y., & Cheng, D. (2023). *Multicultural play therapy: Making the most of cultural opportunities with children. Routledge.* https://www.routledge.com/Multicultural-Play-Therapy-Making-the-Most-of-Cultural-Opportunities-with-Children/Ray-Ogawa-Cheng/p/book/9781032038537

Lumiere Children's Therapy. (n.d.). *At-home occupational therapy activities for children with sensory processing issues.* https://www.lumierechild.com/blog/at-home-occupational-therapy-activities-for-children-with-sensory-processing-issues/

Times of India. (2023). *Why multicultural toys are important for kids.* https://timesofindia.indiatimes.com/life-style/parenting/moments/why-multicultural-toys-are-important-for-kids/articleshow/105787318.cms#:~:text=In%20conclusion%2C%20multicultural%20toys%20are,to%20form%20positive%20self%2Didentities.

CoreWell CEU. (n.d.). 25 play therapy techniques.
https://corewellceu.com/blog/25-play-therapy-techniques

Schaefer, C. E., & Kaduson, H. G. (2010). Implementing play therapy in the schools: Lessons learned. ResearchGate.
https://www.researchgate.net/publication/232525670_Implementing_Play_T herapy_in_the_Schools_Lessons_Learned

The Counseling Palette. (n.d.). 13 thoughtful group therapy activities for all ages.
https://www.thecounselingpalette.com/post/grouptherapyactivities

Association for Play Therapy. (n.d.). Play therapy best practices.
https://cdn.ymaws.com/www.a4pt.org/resource/resmgr/publications/best_p ractices.pdf

Good Play Guide. (2023). The importance of digital play in a child's development.
https://www.goodplayguide.com/blog/the-importance-of-digital-play-in-a-childs-development/

Frontiers in Psychology. (2021). Integrating virtual reality into art therapy with adolescents.
https://www.frontiersin.org/journals/psychology/articles/10.3389/fpsyg.2021 .584943/full

Sunshine Child Counseling. (n.d.). Non-directive vs. directive play therapy – What is the difference? https://sunshinechildcounseling.com/non-directive-vs-directive-play-therapy-what-is-the-difference/

National Center for Biotechnology Information. (2012). Game-based biofeedback for pediatric anxiety and depression. https://www.ncbi.nlm.nih.gov/pmc/articles/PMC3314276/

Quenza. (n.d.). The power of play therapy certification. https://quenza.com/blog/knowledge-base/play-therapy-certification/

Luke, M. (2010). Play therapy techniques that enhance supervision. ResearchGate. https://www.researchgate.net/profile/Melissa-Luke-2/publication/232539665_Supervision_can_be_playful_too_Play_therapy_te chniques_that_enhance_supervision/links/54bdb65e0cf218da9391b7aa/Super vision-can-be-playful-too-Play-therapy-techniques-that-enhance-supervision.pdf

National Center for Biotechnology Information. (2012). The children's play therapy instrument (CPTI). https://www.ncbi.nlm.nih.gov/pmc/articles/PMC3330503/

Australian Play Therapy Association. (2021). APPTA guidelines for ethical play therapy practice. https://appta.org.au/wp-content/uploads/2021/02/Guidelines-for-Ethical-Practices.pdf

Alexander, J. (2023). Trauma-informed play therapy: Attunement is key. https://msjenalexander.com/trauma-informed-play-therapy-attunement-is-key/

American Psychological Association. (2015). Ethical and legal considerations when counselling children. PsycNET. https://psycnet.apa.org/record/2015-57655-005

Foster and Adoptive Family Services. (n.d.). Play therapy for foster children: How does it work? http://foster-adoptive-kinship-family-services-nj.org/play-therapy-for-foster-children-how-does-it-work/

Lester, L. (2010). Play therapist's perspectives on culturally sensitive play therapy. ScholarWorks @ UNO. https://scholarworks.uno.edu/cgi/viewcontent.cgi?referer=&httpsredir=1&article=2424&context=td

Play Therapy Toolbox. (n.d.). BEST online play therapy training websites. https://playtherapytoolbox.com/blog/best-online-play-therapy-training-websites/

Association for Play Therapy. (n.d.). Association for play therapy. https://www.a4pt.org/

Wonders Counseling. (n.d.). 10+ ways to earn income in play therapy. https://wonderscounseling.com/10-ways-to-earn-income-in-play-therapy/

American Psychological Association. (2021). Technological advances and considerations in play therapy. https://apt.digitellinc.com/p/s/technological-advances-and-considerations-in-play-therapy-885

Printed in Great Britain
by Amazon

56017211R00136